NOTES FROM THE ROAD
VOL. IV

DEREK MANSFIELD

Adventure begins when you step through the door

Derek S Mansfield

Shuvvy Press

SHUVVY PRESS LTD
www.shuvvypress.com

First published by Shuvvy Press Ltd, Banbury, England
November 2015
Copyright © Derek Mansfield

Derek Mansfield asserts the moral right
to be identified as the author of this work

A catalogue record for this book is available from
the British Library

ISBN 978-0-9564305-5-7

All rights reserved.
No part of this publication may be reproduced, stored in a
retrieval system, or transmitted, in any form or by any means,
electronic, mechanical, photocopying, recording or otherwise,
without the permission of both the copyright owner and the
above publisher of this book.

Edited by Paddy Tyson
Book design and typesetting by Jo MacDonald at JMDesign
Typeset in Adobe Garamond Pro 10pt
Printed in Wales by Zenith Media Group

Contents

Anxiety Rules	1
A Land that Speaks with Another's Tongue	7
Dogging in the Carpark	13
Handmaidens of Joy	15
The Country with Twenty Three People	23
A Tree Painted Orange and Questionable Sex	25
Chocolate Box Cities, Lolita and lakes	31
Serendipity	35
The Boy Who Ate an Octopus	41
Tax Avoidance and Evasion	45
Revisiting Broken Bones	47
Alphabet Soup	73
Now with Added Navigation	77
Butterflies and Beautiful People	81
Why I Travel by Motorcycle. Alone.	89
Kit for the Journey	93
Your Notes from the Road starts here	99

There are many people I wish to thank, but I cannot list them all. Here are some.

My wife Gabrielle, my family and Natalie my business partner in Ukraine; you've all had to live with my curdled brain for some time. Thank you all for your patience and forbearance.

My friends in the Fellowship who have helped me to stay upright in more ways than one; most especially Keith and Bob.

To all those people who showed me such kindness and generosity on the road. I've changed their names to avoid embarrassment.

The staff at Shuvvy Press for their unerring encouragement.

Petrol station employees and border guards everywhere, especially those who work the night shifts.

Finally, this book is dedicated to my grandson Luke, whose smile and unconditional love is the best reason ever to come home.

Foreword

Don't take life too seriously; you'll never get out alive.

I used to be an average man. In this year, 2015, at the age of sixty nine I am a proud father and grandfather. I'm also physically small and slight in comparison to the giants growing up around me.

I have experienced nineteen careers, many of which were alcohol fuelled.

I speak only one language, English.

I have three terminal illnesses. Only one needs to get me, but I am happier now than I have ever been.

I have found that if you spend a long time alone on a motorcycle, travelling long distances over long periods, there is a very good chance your brain will curdle.

This book is the result of one such curdling.

Anxiety Rules

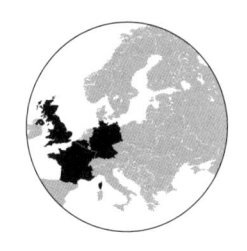

After posting nonsense on Facebook for weeks and finally deciding that delaying my journey would not help a noisome client, someone paid an invoice and I thought… 'Ok, tomorrow would be good'.

The more I travel, the less I plan. The less I plan, the less likely it is that I can get lost. Routes, eventualities and outcomes usually take up eighteen worrisome seconds; but this, the fourth of my long rides, took less.

Onward is the mantra. Onward, the next horizon.

No matter that I have no maps; I have a compass, a recalcitrant phone-powered GPS and some admittedly vague ideas on the trajectory. I had gathered new kit just in case. Two ten litre jerry cans for petrol – lack of which proved such an embarrassment on previous outings – a new stove that could use said petrol as fuel, a pair of on-trend hipster boots and some waterproof socks. And for special evenings out on the road, a pale blue shirt decorated with tiny white flowers. My anxious but ever-loving wife had pressed a packet of dried noodles into a pannier to stave off starvation and a bar of Kit-Kat in the tank bag, secretly stashed.

Thus at this dawn I stood tippy toed, manfully compensating for disadvantaged leg length, straddling the bike trying not to notice the awful sensation of nerves flickering and fingering around in my stomach. I had thought, this year, that as I hadn't told myself when I would be leaving, the tendrils of fear would not have time to attack. But they did.

My wife enquired if I had been to the toilet and with a nodded yes I rolled out of the driveway and wondered if I had packed my passport and if not, how to get past customs.

Minutes later, sun in my eyes; a morning so fresh I can smell the starch as I pass an early commuter's car. I'm shining inside with lands unseen, new friends to make. Fear has gone, the unknown welcomed forward. Small boys startle awake, laying slack jawed in wonder at my passing.

Wives tighten their grip on a husband's arm and older folk smile; five thousand two hundred revolutions of impossibly beating Italian steel create a pitch perfect howl at ninety six point four miles per hour as the beautiful bike projects me across the dawn.

Whoa a bit. Steady as she goes. Twelve hundred kilometres as well as the ferry to make in this present now. Except; too much time fiddling in toilets, fresh fuel to up-fill and a long way to the ferry. So the first of thousands of fuel/mpg/speed/distance computations begin, and the curdle in the brain is spectacularly unleashed.

The passport I had left behind is, by very good fortune, discovered in my tank-bag so I hand it over to the ferry person; no-one else seems interested in it or the length and breadth of my future journey. Perhaps I should have left from the Ace Café with cheering crowds and souped-up sponsors to wobble off and deck it at the first opportunity. Or Twittered ahead for a flashcrowd; big brass band. But you can't organise this in less than eighteen seconds with both hands full of handlebar.

So onto the ferry looking gainfully manly, hoping to catch an eye and tell a good story. To find all ears being filled and me, with Big English eaten, feeling a little queasy. But one man ventured conversation. Mid-thirties, podgy, self-satisfied in a BMW way and I mentioned not that I was a biker of the bravest kind. 'The benefits of forward planning, mobile phones,' he said. I thought 'beam me up'. His provider gave free roaming in nine different countries. Because I didn't have it, I sneeringly asked who wanted to travel in those countries anyway. And felt bad for him when his wife started laughing. And bad for me too, for making cheap laughs and not having the best phone provider.

The reason it was easy to get on this ferry was because it's bound for Dunkirk, not Calais. The town of Dunkirk is fifty kilometres north of Calais by road. But the Dunkirk ferry port is thirty kilometres south of the city, so the advantage by road is negligible. Happy then, that the voyage to Dunkirk only takes one duty-free hour longer than that to Calais. But who am I to judge myself; it's almost proper foreign.

So I vowed, as I stood in the prow, the vanguard of the expeditionary, that this time I would not get lost. Straight and true I would ride, just one thousand more kilometres between me and this night's bed.

And then tried to get in the fast stream as indicated by the weighmaster. Bars high up and thrust through an open car window helping me scrape past the rear of an enormous truck. Sorry, sorry, effusive apologies meaning 'you stupid dick, why did you park there?' And now following a handsome and hirsute black leathered biker, until I was five kilometres short of Calais with words in my helmet, expletives slipping through lips as a thought formed: this bloke's on a round trip or he's lost too.

A glance at the compass, heading due south; a roundabout with third exit taking me east an hour and another two languages before I caught up with ferry travellers who knew where they were going. Now followed by the black clad biker.

At this day's end, five countries and a full twelve hundred kilometres now sliced up, slivers of dim lit road and brain nicely curdled, a kindly clever and beautiful young woman takes me in and smiles like sunrise to ask; 'How are you, it's been years'.

Nataliya; serene grey-greened eyes from the wild country of Ukraine, near the border, at Kharkiv, a city now worried and tugged like a bone by a dog who sits in a President's Palace.

This conversation over dinner with Nataliya and her ex-husband whom I knew from a country other than this, we talked of the past but not of the now, of a country to the east on my route. He remained Russian, she now officially adopted and draped in the EU flag.

I've revered this woman for more than ten years; simultaneously degree'd in three languages and another in computers, science thereof, she guided me through scoping, specifications and contracts in Russian, English and software speak. Then project managed projects when, at a tender twenty one with the courage of a lioness, she said yes to working for me in England. And came and worked and blossomed into beautiful before her brand new husband spirited her off to the country and the city, apartment and room directly on my eastward course to where I now stood hugging her with love of the friendship kind.

To the dairy in the morning to gather in the milk; calves with big brown gentle eyes, cows lowing with content and milk siphoned, chilled, directly from a refrigerated tap filling to the brim your own recycled bottles.

On being chilled there is more of a different kind.

We strolled around her adopted city; pretty in Mittel European, rebuilt, refurbished, reinvented with science and shoes as the beating commercial heart. Replacing... the chill dream of a dictator who built bricks ten metres tall to showcase the March of Marionettes with harsh cries and out-thrust arms. And now, next to a lake it stands; unfinished, dirty, cold and concrete cracked, weed ridden. And if not for millions dead, just somehow very sad, testament to a small moustachioed man who would be God. And failed. Like another small man further east today. Playing out his ego, the lives of others irrelevant to his self-centred hungry needs.

Searching for a restaurant proved to be fun. In this, one of the world's most sophisticated countries, they close the cafés for a month and sally forth abroad. Try that in Mac or high street Starbucks. Four tries it took, of banging on doors and peering through windows to find Mein host awake. And not surly for diners at nine (we close at ten) to open the doors and say food is still served.

Of the steak that I ate? I was glad I was not the person who paid.

A Land that Speaks with Another's Tongue

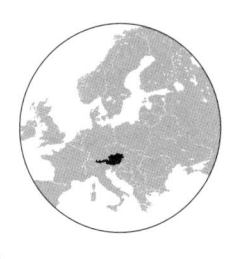

In a previous country, today started well enough; fresh morning, sunshine. Blue skies. An altercation with my host's coffee machine has to be admitted to. The machine won; the second coffee decided against, the open road there waiting, vibrating.

Notes scribbled of apology, endearment and heartfelt thanks, luggage re-strapped, lost for only nine minutes before roads rediscovered, throttle wrapped downward, thundered crescendo and howling east at unmetered speed.

Regrettably, with the clock reading seventeen hundred and five hundred kilometres later, I cowered in a hedge sheltering from torrents of water juiced up by lightning. And then a man rode by on an Enduro into a flood shouting, in English 'Holy Shit. Holy Shit!'

I adjudged this to be normal behaviour in this new country where they spoke not English, but the same language as the country before. Like Scotland and England. Except it was foreign. There were still no clues as to the country; only that roads had worsened considerably.

At one point I was overtaken by an orange truck with the words Motorway Maintenance on the side, bearing Irish licence plates. Could this be part of EU oneness I thought? A flying squad sent to sort out the roadworks? Or had I caught the wrong ferry three days earlier?

The strangeness compounded when an ageing Chevrolet New Yorker sedan also overtook me. The driver, a woman, looked to be in her nineties. Her grip on the wheel was as taut as the lines on her face. She drove so fast and erratically I was convinced she could only be late for an appointment with an Assisted Suicide Clinic; such establishments I believe, plied their trade over the high mountain range to my left. Ten minutes later I overtook her, virtually stopped in the slow lane. Perhaps she didn't need the appointment after all and had simply expired prematurely.

Another hour and I overtook some stationary cows. Painted in vivid primary colours one had the EU insignia plastered across its rump. Had I reached India to see EU sponsored sacred cows roaming the roads at will?

With my singular linguistic prowess you will not be surprised to learn that after the morning's shenanigans, at the next petrol stop I addressed the young man behind the till in Mongolian. I was unsure of his reply; I saw his lips move but my earplugs and helmet prevented me from actually hearing him. As he encouragingly escorted me out of store I was certain that he was not Mongolian, and that this was not Mongolia.

My assurance had its roots in fact; as I re-entered a world of sunshine I was surrounded by hundreds of Japanese people rushing hither and thither like downtown Tokyo. No. Even curdled I knew this wasn't Tokyo. I bowed and smiled and, as I really cannot speak Japanese, tried a bit of Klingon. In moments the tumult stilled and area cleared as all and sundry ran into the bowels of an enormous shiny bus.

I am delighted to tell you, although you may not be that interested, that as I sit at my laptop typing today's tales my bowels are also shiny and clear. Which leads me to believe that although I am somewhere foreign, it is not yet deeply foreign enough.

Onward on the morrow; roads of grey, taupe and occasionally black.

Now with Added Squiggles, but Lacking Lickspittle

I crept, early this morning, from the apartment of a woman whose appetites and manners would have made Falstaff blanch.

Ms. Falstaff, as I shall call her, had a taste for tents rather than dresses to hide her ample form. Moreover, she explained within forty five seconds of meeting, she was of a different sexual persuasion than I. And, she continued, was an activist who had personally befriended members of Bader-Meinhof and in the singular, Bjork. On the upside Ms F had evidently read the collected works of Somerset Maugham and Auberon Waugh.

We'd been to dinner the night before: my mind full of strudel and pastries and thin hammered veal; while she thought of curry, Sri Lankan at that. On arrival at the restaurant and seated outside in a well ordered garden, Ms F ordered dinner which seemingly consisted of eighty percent of the menu. Plate after plate was delivered to the table; she drank large beers and ordered more.

Poppadum's arrived ten deep in a pile. Her hand rose, then skilful and practiced smashed down twice, P'dums quartered, readied for consumption. Which consisted of cramming as much in her mouth as possible whilst still speaking at full volume.

Between handfuls of this and platefuls of that, she spoke of her heritage; Austro-Hungarian, Essex bred. Her story was punctuated by increasingly loud belching, a lifting of the buttock to allow gas to pass and occasional intense scratching where her thighs conjoined. She explained that she thought she may be bi-polar. And as proof of the ailment she demonstrated the relationship with her father; a virtuoso performance of multilingual profanities screamed at the top her voice. With food simultaneously expelled.

I looked around at my fellow diners; they, like me, sitting slack jawed; aghast.

I beckoned the waiter and asked for the bill; on arrival it seemed sufficient to buy a small apartment.

Only now did I discover the true reason for restaurant selection; as the manager hovered whilst I dug deep for cash, Ms F offered her gigging services in his Restaurant to drum up more trade. Being more sophisticated than I, and much wiser, he simply smiled and said 'yes, let's talk about it one day; in the future.'

Walking back to her apartment she pointed out her local and neighbourhood Bar. How nice I opined and steadfastly walked on. Into the apartment and Ms F, in full lip licking mode, announced that she must take her cat for a walk. I agreed, as long as she went on her own. And that was the last I saw of her, for at dawn there was still no sign.

This singular night was enough; and although it was more interesting than talking to myself in Pidgin Swahili (I have a terrible accent), I could take no more. I mention this only in passing because as luck would have it she lived very near to the centre of the city I was in.

I do not usually sight-see the obvious; but because I was lost and picking my way between cobblestones and tramlines with one eye on the road, another on the compass and the third on the hieroglyphics that pass for directional signs, I found myself outside a 19th Century equivalent of the O2 Stadium; an Opera House. No singing, too early, but it was indeed a handsome building.

When lost I usually turn left, then left and then sharp right. This was taught to me by a recalcitrant Satnav voice. In this case, as I had no idea where I was or where I was going – apart from a general northerly heading – it made little difference; but I did it anyway. Which led me this morning, in a roundabout fashion, to a market crowded with shoppers buying sausages and beer. Actually, considering the size of the aforesaid populace it was probably just an outside outsized breakfast bar.

I left, left, righted again and to my delight was surrounded by nothing except an enormous square, at the centre of which were fountains and monumental soldiers.

Left, left, right and I was following a column of commercial trucks. You know the drill. When in doubt follow the trucks. They'll get you into a city and out of it, but not always in the order that you want.

I had been riding now for about fifteen minutes and the lack of caffeine and nicotine were having a markedly deleterious effect on my navigation. In truth, and even with luck, it still took an hour before I managed to find a café that sold petrol on the correct side of the road. The architecture was motorway chic and the staff apparently employed especially for their lack of comprehension of the international argot, namely English.

Ms F, who gigs (I still have no idea what this means) between two adjacent foreign countries including the one I met her in, earlier informed that said unnamed country did not encourage guest workers to do menial work; instead they employed illiterate native menials on a job for life basis.

It doesn't take an M.Sc. in Economics to understand what happened to the service ethic. In Britain of course we proudly take any foreign degree'd person and train them to make tea. But here in Ms. Falstaff's backyard the hired help lacked sufficient lickspittle, preferring it would seem, to grunt.

So I grunted back; albeit with a refined Kazakh accent.

Finished with coffee and employment law I regained my seat and rode into a miracle. I crossed an entire language zone without getting a word wrong. I achieved it mainly because the country was small and I only needed to fill the tank once. At the petrol station, tank freshly brimmed with benzene, I walked to the pay counter, caught a server's eye and said 'Dva' meaning pump number two.

The server said 'Da' and the transaction was over. It possibly helped that although I suspected I was not in Russia, speaking Russian and simultaneously holding up two fingers was a fairly normal occurrence.

The added squiggles were everywhere. Pert bottoms, road signs, longer limbs and, as I crossed the border where rosy-cheeked old ladies sat selling apples, a man waved his penis at me. I nodded gracefully and gave a flaccid wave back. I have to say it looked like jolly good fun but I didn't really have time to stay and chat.

Onward then, with the squiggles giving way to slashed consonants and a total incomprehension of exchange rates, to the hotel room in which I sit writing this. I think I may have got a room bargain. But I doubt it.

Dogging in the Carpark

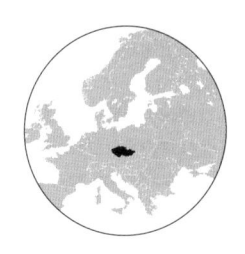

What an interesting country this is.

At a motorway café an attractive man sporting a beard and wearing red socks arrived on a bicycle. Alighting, he walked up to three other men, who were not wearing any socks at all, spoke to them briefly in squiggle with some slashed consonants and then proceeded to snog them all in the continental manner.

This was very interesting to me as I thought dogging was done in car parks in the woods. Were the red socks a secret introduction, a code? I would have asked, but cognisant that I was wearing tan brogue boots their interest may have been unduly piqued. I refrained from introducing myself and continued on my way.

The journey unfolded through pretty towns and villages; even the meanest had bright painted houses, the architecture bearing the unmistakable stamp of an Imperial past. A fine mist had translated itself into a slithery surface although the roads were in good condition. I did give thanks to the manufacturers of wet weather clothing and especially my new purchases of waterproof socks and pull over boots. The marvellous thing was that every time I struggled them on, the rain stopped. After two roadside clothing changes and no rain, I was dry but exhausted. Naturally when I continued in leathers and denims it poured. After a while I began to smell; it's probably why no-one wished to speak to me in their native language, or any other language come to that.

With the compass pointing vaguely north I considered that I was making good progress. However having no map I couldn't actually measure distance apart from the slashed consonant road signs and diminishing numbers. So I may have been travelling in circles but the roads excited and I was thoroughly enjoying motorcycle fun.

Occasionally enormous traffic jams blighted progress. The EU is still ladling billions into central Europe and, apart from establishing white water rapids in city centres, more money continues to ramp up the road building programme. For which I am grateful.

Actually I got lost in this very country a couple of years ago whilst seeking a route to Mongolia. Back then the motorway expired with no warning and the Satnav gave up in anguish. Eerily now, I recognised a consonated word and realised I was in the same city, but two years and twenty kilometres further on.

Having skirted another five kilometre jam I decided to find a flop house and arrived instead at a surprisingly smart hotel which appeared to have a connection with the fried chicken joint next door. Room established, chicken digested, sleep came easily.

Handmaidens of Joy

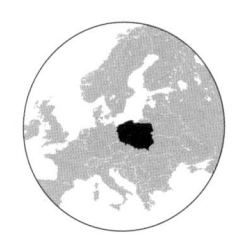

Another perfect morning and the yen to travel the national roads, avoiding the capital city.

As I rode on, more English words appeared on the roadside billboards. It seemed to me that the deeper into a country the denizens are subjected more to the use of English in advertising to give the illusion of sophistication. Strangely I have yet to see this in Merrie England. Russian posters in Aylesbury would surely terrify the population.

Tootling throttle, birds singing; and there in the wooded clearings stood the Handmaidens of Joy plying their ageless trade. A perfect prial; blonde, brunette and redhead. They wore short skirts that fluttered in the breeze, skimped blouses and a selection of jackets from denim to leather. I know it may be strange for pretty young women to walk through the forest in knee length, high heeled boots so early in the morning, but it was the make-up that advertised most. Bright red lips, fluttering lashes; could have been Ascot but the sun was shining too much. And they weren't wearing hats.

'How convenient for commuters' came the thought. A quickie before reaching the office? Like a good breakfast it could set-up a man for the day. Me, you ask? Well no, not really. I don't usually eat breakfast.

Having no local currency I dine only in petrol stations when travelling as, ninety nine percent of the time, they accept credit cards. Mid-afternoon, having passed yet another bevy of Handmaidens, I pulled into an outpost of the global oil economy, filled the tank and, apropos of nothing, answered yes when the smiling girl behind the till asked me if I would like a hot dog.

A small crowd had gathered around the bike and began nudging each other on my approach. I struck a pose in my handcrafted brown leather jacket, a la café racer. The crowd dispersed and it was only then I realised the mustard from the hot dog was gliding down my jacket like a brown and yellow Jackson Pollock.

The last Soviet Ice Cream Parlour

I stood peering into a hole in the ground surrounded by giants. I had stood in this self-same spot twenty two years previously when the hole was a railway station, and the people seemed considerably smaller.

I have a theory about cat food. It's so nutritious that domestic cats are growing inexorably larger; by the end of the century they will be the size of tigers. With people it is the same; Western Europe and the USA will probably sink below the waves because of the gargantuan stature of its people.

This city, I discovered whilst walking later, is the one that spent EU money on a killer white-water rafting course right in the centre. I say killer because two people joined Neptune in eternity when they first tried it out. The city was also spending money on a brand new railway station but so far only constructed a hole; as a consequence on my stroll I recognised nothing. No station, no ageing Soviet hotel. Nothing.

My host, a most avuncular man with a sharp dry sense of humour and a Walter Matthau delivery, said all Soviet cities used to look very similar. Was I sure it was this city I had arrived at all that time ago?

I knew it was. It still had two vowels, nine consonants and two zeds. As unpronounceable then as now.

In truth, the city had changed beyond belief. My first visit was for business just around the time of Perestroika. The offices were relentless grey concrete streaked with rust, broken windows and the ceaseless tympani of latchless iron doors. Inside, and as a foretaste of what was to happen to the nation, everything was smart white desks, black leather chairs and potted plants.

I couldn't find that old office of course. Concrete was now painted Armani mute with Bauhaus stencilled numbers. The city centre with river, churches – one uprated to Cathedral status – an opera house and a theatre set upon teeming gleaming cobbled squares with enough cafés to make Parisians feel jealous, was simply stunning.

What of Walter? Here was a guy who took history, sex, drugs and rock and roll seriously. We repaired, in the evening, to visit the city's bars. Plentiful the bars, full of handsome men, some even with hipster style beards, and tall beautiful girls in short dresses; none showing over indulgence in alcohol.

Finally to a bar converted from a riverside warehouse comprising a warren of small rooms. Four stories high with a river view on each, ancient wooden beams, equally the doors, floors gnarled and uneven, the top floor with the added excitement of a wooden bridge crossing an atrium below. Quality blues, real R&B and vintage rock 'n' roll different in each room. Low lighting, low couches and low coffee tables, the whole could be a set for a modern medieval film. It was of course, brimming with the beautiful people and no place for the likes of me. But we were there because Walter had been led to believe that a man from America would be present with drugs in his pocket. Donated free.

A cast of four

The man from America hailed originally from Pakistan; his mother had an affair and was slated for death by stoning. Gathering her son and a good deal of money she ran from the country and reached, circuitously New York, New York. Her son, with a change of name, enrolled in medical school, she erasing their past as the husband still sought her religious but honourable death. He is tall, this doctor, slim and dark with glossy black hair, twinkling dark brown eyes and sharp, if accented, repartee – an exotic in a land of tall blondes.

Next is the woman. Thirties, tall even for her race, intelligent and blonde, wide grey eyes and a wider white smile, amusing, travelled, a teller of good tales, university background and a disciple, she told me, of Cyndi Lauper's 'Girls just wanna have fun.'

Third cast member is my friend, the aforesaid Walter. Walter also has good height, well-built though tending to pudge, late thirties and interestingly handsome in the craggy Matthau model. He too has a university education but does not work. His father left him properties which provide a reasonable income and the reason to calculate daily whether he should improve a property here in order to charge more rent or sell another to re-invest. He thinks long and often, takes walks and drinks beer, but no action is taken on the property empire.

And lastly, with a walk-on part of a passing stranger and diarist, is me.

Three scenes and a final act

Scene one: Walter and the doctor from New York are both, understandably, in heat for the woman. No permanent relationship is sought. Just heat and now.

Dialogue is in English to be inclusive for the doctor and me; but I tire rapidly for, though I share the male interest, I am short, a pensioner and happily married.

Scene two: It is past my bedtime and after an hour of sipping cola listening to the jousting and measuring of members, I decide to leave. Walter has no money for the buying of more drinks. I give him the cash that I have left, he gives me the keys to his car. I leave the bar and drive, smiling, the four kilometres to his apartment.

Scene three – which is told in Walter's words and I repeat as hearsay: More drinks are taken, the participants are starting to glow. The rumours of drugs appear to be correct; Ecstasy or some derivative is to be served, no need for prolonged seduction, the mood swing and enjoyment virtually guaranteed. The good doctor dispenses to himself and the girl; they glow even more. Walter's share of medication has little effect, except he feels tired. And more tired and seemingly unable to speak.

The doctor beams and with a tight grip on our lady's bottom leaves the bar, smiling all the while. Walter realising he has been slipped pills for sleeping, not sensual action, staggers to the street and discovers simultaneously all the cash, his and mine, has been spent on the foreplay booze. He has to walk, as taxi drivers prefer money to solemn promises of payment to come.

Four hours later, the final act of this piece: Walter sits at my bedside relating his tale, having walked from the bar at an average speed of one kilometre an hour. He is not particularly upset, he tells me, as his long term girlfriend may not have approved of additional congress with others off stage. But he no longer has trust in wily exotic dispensers of American made Medicaid.

Most mornings – and I was lucky enough to accompany him once – Walter went, rain or shine, to the last Soviet ice cream parlour in the city. The Soviet managers, a man in his fifties and a wife somewhat younger, had embraced Perestroika, taking ownership and changing nothing in a quarter of a century.

The parlour is in a Stalin architectured part of the city; Soviet art deco buildings, high ceilinged low rise blocks with small shops built in at the base. Today, and in perfect original and not retro restyled, the only ice cream to eat was the chocolate. Or so said Walter. It is the same that he ate in Soviet times when he was a boy living in an apartment just a few minutes' walk away.

It's true I think.

I had coffee, which tasted of acorns.

Of Oil and Elasticated Knickers

The order of the day was fixing of the drip; an oil leak that the mechanic who changed the fluids had failed to correct. Needless to say the mechanic was me; enough is already said.

Full of mechanical fear I rode to a bike shop. Thoughts of cross-threaded filters and chewed up metal had been billowing around my brain for the past two thousand miles. The qualified mechanic in the bike shop wheeled the Guzzi to the lift and raised it on high; so simple if you know what you are doing and have the strength to do it.

I stood by with a brand new oil filter, special tools – oil filter removal of – and a litre of 10w60 carried all the way from England for emergencies like this. I pressed forward to help, to assist. The mechanic who knew what he was doing gave two turns to a bolt.

No drip.

Nor would he accept any money.

Humbled, I rode on to explore beautiful fresh-blacked roads with curves and lakes beside them, shiny in sunlight, greened by the forest. With the coming of evening, loss of light and a new border twenty kilometres hence, I chose the Hotel Hanka.

Four years ago, riding my rock 'n roll cruiser on the long road to Kurdistan I took a break and crossed the Black Sea, with the bike, on a ferry. I shared my cabin with a dark haired beauty, a radio journalist from Czech, because she was trying to avoid an overweight Bulgarian woman with body odour and very bad breath. My new journalist friend was slim and well mannered; her name was Hanka. Here today, near this new border where I knew not one hotel from another I chose her namesake.

A mistake.

The Red Star adorning reception should have given me warning, but no.

Too tired, I watched the receptionist's lips move but understood nothing. Years of night service had drained her face of colour. And years of hotel food in the staff canteen had added several inches to her girth and wobbly jowls to her neck. In short, and she was that too, her presence and demeanour were decidedly unprepossessing.

Dressed in a tired white cotton applique blouse, black skirt and, when she bent down to reveal large elasticated knickers, she lost my interest and her authority. The authority was practiced; she wanted me to move my motorcycle to the open and unsecure carpark at the back of the hotel in order to allow more blacked out black four-by-fours and other flashy junk to fill front of house.

I explained in Klingon (always a last resort) that for reasons of Starship security this could not be done.

She was to sit at her monitor all night and discourage criminals and vagabonds from touching my machine. I think she may have studied Klingon in her off-duty time because, when I came down in the morning she was still there and so was my motorcycle. I gave her a joyful smile, she looked at me grey faced with tired red eyes; I went to breakfast because it was included in the price.

The Country with Twenty Three People

Ten days or so ago, in a land that looks like Norfolk, only bigger, they had lost the slashes and squiggles; but here they dot the E.

The distinguishing factor, apart from the lack of lakes and green forests, is the presence of grey cars and white peaked hats; no traffic cameras here; the return of the traffic cop.

It's 34°C and emptier than a Sonoran sauna; perhaps the nation has heatstroke or immigrated to England.

A petrol station; confusing cashless pumps and three short dark girls vend coffee with not so much as a smile between them. What happened to the flashing teeth, clean limbed blonde giantesses of yesterday?

And why did I think the baklava I ordered, two thousand miles from its original home, would taste like anything more than straw.

In the three hours it took to traverse the county on arrow straight roads I saw twenty three people: Four cops, three petrol station waitresses, thirteen people in the distance and three walking men.

And that is all there is to say about the land of the dotted E.

Until later.

A Tree Painted Orange and Questionable Sex

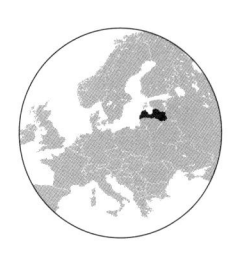

Within twenty minutes of the border the land has changed; pine and birch forest, lakes and sweeping bends on first class roads.

A sort of cedilla has attached itself to the Latin characters on road signs. These cedillas appear to have curtailed the sending of texts; at least I cannot communicate with my upcoming hostess and her family.

The sheet of paper I have been using as a map is now soaked with petrol. I had a short argument with a petrol pump; the pump won and all hope of compass points and town names had totally disappeared.

Many decades earlier I was a Royal Navy sailor on a nuclear-powered missile submarine; we had an early version of satellite navigation but sometimes, and especially underwater, it was difficult to determine a precise location. In those days I served as the Navigation Officer's right-hand man; when we were lost it was my duty to shake broken chicken bones on the table and try to work out our position. This was not always effective and I remain jolly pleased that we fired few missiles based on chicken bone projections.

The 'map' was my last touch of England so I was reluctant to throw it away. Also, I had five litres of good English petrol in a jerry can bungeed to the seat; the map could be used as touch paper if I had to defend myself from men in red socks, giants or off-course nuclear missiles.

The countryside was green and yellow and occasionally spotted with villages with festivals and fêtes in full spate; none of which, I regret, in my honour.

I passed a tree painted orange in a field of green and then observed another quaint local custom. On a rare flat and barren section of road next to the tree of orange a petrol station winked its prices and I pulled in to let the motorcycle feed. About fifty metres east of the station a solitary bush was the recipient of a liberal effusion of urine from a man who stood before it. Completing his task he waved his wand with great enthusiasm. Then another man stepped out from behind the bush, smiling.

Another great country I thought, and waved to them both as I passed.

Finally I remembered that each country had its own customs and phone networks. I cleverly registered my phone on the cedilla country network and presto… it worked. Isn't it always the technology that trips you up?

My lovely hostess spoke Cedillenglish and explained that although I was a hundred kilometres away and heading in the wrong direction, they would be delighted to see me. And arrive I did a brisk two hours later to meet Maria, her son, her father, mother and sister. And an enormous dog that spent most of the next two days trying to hump me.

Maria, greeting me at the gate of the pebbled drive to her hand-built home, is short and peers through round reading glasses. Glasses removed she can see, and I can too, that she has a blue eyed sweet oval face and a classic Slavian figure; small breasts, slim waist, wide hips, slim toned arms and perfect legs as revealed in a smart, and short, low haltered yellow dress.

Her son runs to wave and smile; friendly and inquisitive. Later she tells me, for her son is dark whilst she has lighter colouring, he is the product of a short but wondrous union with a smart talking South American she met whilst working in London at a well-known chain of sandwich bars. Alcohol, loneliness and sweet promises helped begat the boy. He is beautiful and bright, well loved by the family.

Her family is not without some earlier misadventures of a more adult kind. Her father, physically strong, suntanned and handsome even in his pensioned years, has an illness similar to my own but his untreated; he often drinks to the edge of insanity.

Years ago, with his own hands, he rebuilt the family home renting the top floor to his mistress. His wife, outraged and insulted, still had little choice. To leave would make her homeless and penniless with two school-age children. So she lived with the alcoholism and shame until the mistress was dismissed. Today alcohol is hidden away.

In fact, as she told me at nine in the morning, drinking a large glass of local red wine – her husband away at the dentist – there is no alcohol ever in the house. It is hidden in the garden for her sole and exclusive use as the husband, once tasted, cannot stop drinking for days and sometimes weeks.

I gave her, I hope, some comfort and insight from my own illness in the past.

As to questionable sex?

'It's not you', said Maria with a smile when I queried my sex appeal and large dogs – he, the dog, humps anything on two legs. Sexual preferences aside, I lock my bedroom each night and ignore the excited breathing and scratching at the door; and especially in the bagna with sauna attached.

I can see Mermaids Sitting on Rocks

My second day in Cedillaland and I'm invited to the seaside. In fact this sea connects nine countries but from where I am I can see only one.

But I can see mermaids sitting on rocks into whose underwear I would gladly have jumped had not my arse slipped south resembling long ridden, corrugated roads, and a woman, my wife, scheduled to read these words sometime, on current projection, in the future.

Regrettably mermaid watching was too quickly terminated; it was off to the family farm. Maria milked cows when her grandmother was still in charge but the cows have gone and what remains is a beautiful pastoral idyll that the family visit in summer.

Note idyll, not idle. Water is still drawn from the stream and old style mellow yellow electrics light the manse. And a wonderful vintage Zil truck that I doubt will start very soon.

So we drew water from the stream, showered from a bucket with holes, cooked pasta on a Soviet stove and watched the universe wheel through the heavens.

To reach the farm a country track; loose shingle, sand and crossed over ruts, always a nightmare for me. Although I have ridden thousands of kilometres on roads that most would consider off, I still have a great deal of fear; especially when a passenger is pillion perched.

Three times I travelled the ten kilometre road, pillioned and safe. Each time I asked the gods of the road to keep me safe, and they did.

As I left in the morning, no pillion now, I made the same prayer that was once more answered kindly.

Except this time, after reaching fine firm tarmac I dropped myself and machine into a hole I hadn't noticed before.

Men in cars flagged down for assistance, the first with his wife even older than me. So a second was stopped as well. Three men straining and grunting as a wife looked on cheering, uprighted the bike; to my surprise, damage free.

Eternal love and gratitude exchanged and off to the next horizon. And a note to self underlining, be careful what you pray for.

Chocolate Box Cities, Lolita and Lakes

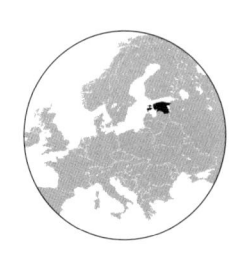

Road signs don't normally bother me.

They're only useful if you have a destination. So a language with twenty three letters should be simple you'd think, like English. But no… there are nine unused characters that make cameo appearances when you have a destination and you're trying to read signs.

For once, by choice, I've arrived in a capital city; as I'd been told that pretty cities festoon this region one wouldn't hurt; and it didn't. Laura, my newest hostess, is both generous and honest, great conversation full of smart one-liners, and a huge and beautiful smile and appetite for life. She does long road trips with friends to dangerous places, enjoying escapades and adventures en-route. One of these friends, the charming Christina, travels long distances with her Kuwaiti husband in a Ural sidecar combination including England to here before me. I love the people I meet on the road!

To the old town with Laura and Christina to view antiquities and architecture all neatly assembled, painted in pastels for chocolate box imprints.

The main observation; a Russian ghetto with second class citizens drunk on the streets. 'They like it this way' explained Laura – a lawyer. 'We encourage them to leave by not giving jobs as they're unqualified for anything except menial tasks. But even unemployed they say it's better than being in Russia.'

Interesting. Especially as thirty percent of the population can claim to be Russian.

Of the war in Ukraine? Send in the troops the locals say. 'We fought them and won in '72; let the Russian Paradise stay where it is.'

Bars and restaurants were filling as dusk painted pastels with pink; we repaired to a smart local restaurant untrammelled by tourists; and then home. To meet Lolita, better known as Bella Meow (sic)

Dark, beautiful, waved hair highlighted blue and elegant feet, usually Doc Marten'd, she studies in Paris for a degree in Sexuality, Gender and simultaneously, Psychology. And although she's still twenty, she knows a lot more than I about those things. And told me.

She's STD free, likes both girls and boys, posts pictures on Facebook and discusses, at length, on hooking as a noble art, anal sex and how best to enjoy it. Most especially describing nude modelling in chains, in live Parisian exhibits. And her jealous same-age friends back home who could not legally drink. And all of this whilst wearing bits of string masquerading as underwear, sitting crossed legged akimbo and leaning backward to push the rest of her forward.

So I asked, as one does, about the large tattoos at the top of the back of her thighs.

'By Nabokov' she said, 'Fire Of My Loins, from Lolita'.

I nodded, agreed and admired, retiring alone to my bed.

In the morning prepared to leave for a lake three hours to the east; one border still in twenty three letters, the other, in another, ruled by a man of small stature known to be aggressive.

With few petrol stations en-route I finally confirmed that the range of my tank was two hundred and fifty five kilometres before it ran dry. And run out it did as I glided five metres to a stop next to a Euro95 pump. To pay in advance, where, for once

I knew how much petrol was needed.

Another hour of metalled forest roads and the lake was huge and calm with cabins nearby where I'd been promised a four poster bed.

The food was good, plentiful and inclusive and so, had I wished, was the booze.

For added entertainment about seventy lively late twenties people from at least nine nations travelled here to show me how to party in a north Nordic way.

The promise of the bed, as made by the lawyer, wasn't quite fulfilled; I pondered the difference between four posters and a tent, lawyers and lies, as I lay that night on hard earth listening to naked Finns cavorting in water and the blue-lit saunas, guests for the use of, free.

On the morrow six hundred kilometres of road awaited, so I put plugs in my ears and, sadly ignoring two new female tent mates who arrived in the night with 'Hello', drifted off to sleep.

Serendipity

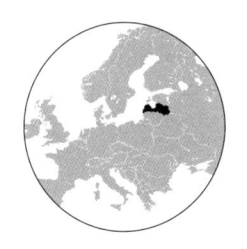

Today's goal was a city to the south six hundred kilometres hence. With the engine sounding a tad discomforted and tappity, a decision is taken to ride country roads rather than banging down a motorway.

And what roads they were. Long narrow straights through deep green forest, curves and sweepers past lakes and rivers sparkling in sunshine; stops for coffee and cake.

Biker bliss ruled.

And then, traversing the ripped up road on the outskirts of a very small town, the sound and feel of an engine hiccupping; No! No! I shouted in my helmet, not now!

But the engine misheard, misfired and then stopped, kilometres from nowhere on single track road.

The heavens opened and splashed thick juicy water as I inspected the... well whatever I was supposed to inspect when the engine won't fire, oil drips on the road and the wind in the trees laughs at your plight.

Cars swish by enjoying the spray. I stand and pray... and a biker appears in the gloom of this wet afternoon. No need to wave down, Jacob pulls up alongside and says clearly, uncluttered and in my own language, 'Do you need any help?'

'Fucked' I say, demonstrating my wide and knowledgeable mechanical vocabulary. 'Engine, it fucked.'

'Can you speak English?' smiled Jacob.

Holding back tears I watch the clear-eyed youthful Jacob switch switches on and off, check fuses, prod wires and determine an electrical fault, but alas, no roadside fix is possible.

'Do you know of a nearby service station' I inquired of this man who lived in the next country down.

'Not ahead as I've never been there' he replied, 'but the town I just left is large and skilled people can probably be found.' And then he told me the name of the town. It's what? I cried and on repeat I said but I stayed there just last week.

It's the town where mermaids sit on rocks!

As my phone had developed an empathy with the engine and handily died, I used Jacob's to call the amazing Maria and excitedly explain I had crossed borders and roads with no idea as to where I was but she was living almost next door. And remembered to say; 'Do you know any motorcycle service shops?'

A good thing this wasn't England and that Maria didn't know that mechanics of any kind don't work late on a Saturday afternoon. 'Give me ten minutes' she said with conviction.

And ten minutes to the second she called Jacob back and said 'A van is on its way'.

With more road to reap Jacob shook my hand, carefully accepted my card with a smile and roared off to his next horizon.

I waited alone.

Rain. Grey. Very English.

Soggily smoking and for something to do I looked up the road, then down the road with no clear idea of which was which. Listened to the rain tattooing my helmet and gently kicked my tent, spare petrol can and sundry other items removed to access electrical inspections, now stacked with no neatness on the verge.

Then in the distance, lights. Engines thrumming and a cavalcade of cars. Handbrake turns and a truck that swoops to a halt; dark and muscled men spill out laughing and smiling. 'We help you, no problems, we bikers.'

Ah joy! God's own people arrived to assist and roll up the bike into a van designed for double glazing, glass dumped for the rescue attempt.

We set off with speed; the driver explaining he has to work in another country tonight so swift is the card to play. The owner behind me tells me in English of his business in the mountains of France; building ski lodges for rich dilettantes with more money than sense.

'I take all their money' he whoops in glee, 'so help bikers like you!'

And gently skid into a gravelled backyard with advertising boards adorned with Lawn Mower Repairs in a language other than mine, the man standing as previously and urgently requested to standby for repairs for an English.

Cars empty once more, handshakes and manhugs then multiple displacement of gravel from tyres and a scattering to other lands as a smiling Maria appears and translates 'Fucked' to the Lawn Mower Man.

He smiles back.

We leave in Maria's very fine Ford through the re-welcomed streets of her town to re-unite with family, now friends. And the dog that humps all in sight.

Cross Dressing in the Land of the Cedillas

I can feel and smell a man's hot breath on my neck. The arms and neck of my t-shirt have been ripped away; I am wearing a woman's very tight trousers.

In front of me bass incantations; to the side a woman's voice and music swelling.

Yesterday was reasonably simple.

The bike coughed and died. A two-wheeled Samaritan rescued me by telling me I was in the land of the mermaids; the mermaid arranged a lawn mower man to urgently fix and repair.

And then to a birthday party infested with infants one of whom poured piping hot country coffee over me, my clothes and my ego.

Country coffee is new to me. I have carried continuously an Aeropress filter coffee maker forty thousand kilometres through mountains and steppes of Eastern Europe and far Central Asia which, with pre-ground Lavazza in a handy sized vacuum packed bag, I brew fresh and delicious coffee anywhere, anytime.

Country coffee is brewed by dumping the grounds in a cup, adding hot water and waiting for gravity to settle the flavours. It works very well. We live, we learn. But when it's dumped on your clothes with your body inside – even filling my on-trend shoulder bag to boot, and boots – it does stain quite badly.

So off with kecks at very high speed – it's the heat of hot coffee that forces this move – to change into… Ah. The lawn mower man has my spare jeans locked tight in his lock up.

So it's a pair of the mermaid's very tight jeans to cover my corrugations, as I stand in church on Sunday with a man leaning over my backless, but also on-trend, NYC outrageously turquoise t-shirt, breathing hot breath on my neck.

From church to cocktails in the Town (a fine Sunday tradition) and thence to the Tea House of the August Moon, so named because the Mermaid's father built an octagonal tea house and now the huge waxed yellow of the August moon shines on as we sit, the mermaid, the sister and mother in the garden, secretly drinking drink to be hidden from the father. Who doesn't have a problem with drink; more, that once he starts there isn't enough drink left in the world to finish.

Morning bright and shiny and it's one last hump with the dog before we're off to the lawn mower emporium, small money changing hands as the fried melted cable and fuse for the generator are hung like a trophy and hugs and eyes misting and glistening with the compass heading south and no village roads, for the moment, with which to contend.

The Boy Who Ate an Octopus

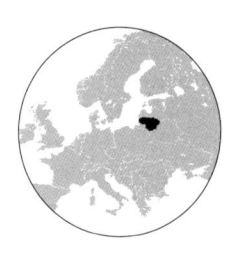

'Octopus please', said the eleven year'd boy from Kansas.

And why not, thought I. The last time I was in this country there were only twenty three people; now here's a small Yank completely conversant with cephalopods. I tried some: delicious; which was good because I could no longer afford to eat.

I was sitting with the boy, his aunt and her friend in a beautiful country house, hotel and restaurant formerly inhabited by rich folk dressed in poor cloth.

An Italian architect engaged to create a slightly smaller version of a domed Roman miracle worked assiduously for the Glory of God, and his servants, now morphed as monks and monkettes.

As the servants were paying, the architect designed, for an additional fee, a New Model Village in which the wealthy could piously sit, praying forgiveness of the sins they committed whilst enriching themselves on Earth.

A thick damask tablecloth, gleaming tableware and glittering glasses were doing their best to belittle the writer's oil stained and road dirt-blackened finger nails as I pointed my forefinger at the menu. The dish I had chosen was selected for the single thing I could read; the price.

I am no longer aware of what I ate and mimed unconcerned as the waiter brought three more knives and three more forks in order for us all to sample octopus with salad on the side. With much clattering of cutlery to show my good manners and the taking of a cephalopodic sliver the tasting, in moments, came to end. The Kansan Kid wolfed down the rest in fewer seconds than he has years of age.

From America he'd travelled, the nephew of my good lady host. And told me on good authority that water from the Himalayas contained microbes so fearsome that they ate body and blood from the inside out. Of Ebola I said nothing. Whilst he continued recounting the Island Of Dolls, where hangings happen daily, I wondered what they taught in primary schools in America. And of the American Mosque to which his Russian Islamic father now sends him.

He was voluble, wholesome, blonde, corn and octopus fed in that mid-American way; his aunt exotic and most handsome with more than a high cheek-boned tint of Tatar blood and smiling tiger eyes. We'll call her, for this story, Lucia. Which is close to her delightful, but for me unpronounceable, name.

Lucia is an architect who spends most of her time, not on design, but on completing competing forms to save the heritage of a wall, a street or a city and in the current case, wheelchair access for prisoners in a prison where one hundred per cent of inmates walk with a spring in their step. 'EU', she says wryly, 'they makes us to do this, always'.

There are three hundred million EU taxpayers say I. Take the money and send an assassin to the prison with orders to break legs and justify expenses.

Next day in the morning, with Kansas, Lucia and her friend on a guided tour of my second tourist city; but this is more to my taste. Not yet completely chocolate boxed; plaster falls from walls revealing centuries old pink bricks. Tourists yes; cafes, restaurants and workshops set on cobbled streets with people working, making, mending, cars, bikes, stoves and iron and wood hammering, sawing, banging and drilling. The good sound of a proper community; not just ferris wheeled with candyfloss filling the cracks.

Lucia's apartment; outside still a Soviet block of the Kruschev design. Inside bright, elegant with an architect's touch and taste and talk over dinner of Buddhism and Zen with homegrown tomatoes and courgettes straight from the village. Outside, a thunderstorm crashing, rivers of rain, me thankful for being safe off the bike: of the fear from the east; one quarter of the population, mostly in drink, ill-educated for lack of trying, waiting for their human rights and language to be upheld with the guns of tanks. Sabres rattling, NATO flying fighters in continuous exercise understood with the folk-born more than willing to fight than wear the yoke again.

Of Perestroika and hardship, and continuing recovery, only half the government are crooks. But democracy firm, and opportunities abound.

Of beauty and nature and mountains and sand dunes for filming in the west by the sea, as yet unseen by me when in the morning I load the bike and with gentle hugs and genuine regrets, a slow riding exit say 'A bientot.'

Which I mean. For I will go back.

Tax Avoidance and Evasion

The compass is marked due south for seven hundred kilometres then left a bit and I slip, albeit with a Moto Guzzi roar, into a country previously visited. I know this because I recognise, but cannot pronounce, the slashed consonants on road signs.

I elected to take this route because the country on my left has links with Mr Putin's regime and charges heavily for visas, should I wish to visit. I do not wish to pay the visa tax and I do wish to avoid or evade anything or anywhere that promotes the Putin horror show.

In front of me better roads than those to the west and north; but better roads means no verges for the handmaidens of joy and other sundry amusements to gawp at. Instead I enjoy the accelerated speed, absence of tolls and policemen and note that houses in this country are considerably larger than the last.

Indeed Soviet rule has been absent here for thirty years; corruption is less than the next country I am to visit and it shows, clearly, in the economy and the national infrastructure.

For the journey and energy Snickers and sausage eaten, Coca-Cola imbibed and on to the border, smiling, nodding and omitting to purchase worthless insurance; for which I will pay, heavily, later.

Revisiting Broken Bones

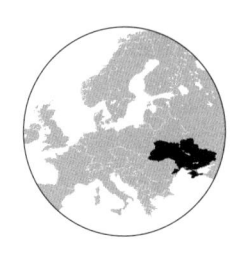

I visited this city in Volumes I, II and III; it is the city that changes a journey into adventure. In Volume III I broke two ribs as across wet cobbles I slid, with the Guzzi, underneath a bright yellow bus. A crowd had quickly gathered; a female shout, voiced in English, of assurance and I and the bike were picked up, carried to the roadside, with ambulances arriving, police and bus drivers bribed to forget and me transported to an apartment where the good folk held a biker party that very night to celebrate my entry to the country.

So I met these good people again at a petrol station two years and ten kilometres out to avoid the city and the cobbles except by foot, the next day, to a bar before noon where a password was given and entry allowed.

There is further test of veracity. Standing in the dark brick-built vault at the entrance guarded by a Kalashnikov-carrying uniformed man, we are given a patriotic drink containing patriotic alcohol and asked a patriotic question. If we do not drink, or reply wrongly, or reply with an incorrect accent, a Red Star will appear on our foreheads. And should the red star appear we will be taken aside and shot.

I have an allergy to alcohol so I am excused; I also failed the question, but my English accent was approved. I am somewhat surprised. For this is the country which surrendered the fourth largest arsenal of nuclear weapons in the world on the solemn and binding promise that if aggression was threatened then my country and America would protect them.

We didn't.

The promise broken with nary a thought. The lily livered politicians in London too friendly with the whispers from the bankers who launder billions of corrupt dollars from the very aggressor that threatens.

The reason given for the onset of war? Unlike other countries with two languages the supposed banning of one gave leave to another country to start a war, which continues. The media war already won and invaders stride the streets in the East.

In fact; whilst sitting in this very bar I read the story of Mr Putin's press conference promoting the Russian re-armament programme of seven hundred billion dollars. When questions were called a brave Siberian stood up and said 'This talk of billions to be spent is all very well, but I cannot afford a car.'

To which Mr Putin asked 'Why would you want a car in Siberia when there are no roads?' his accidental irony missed in his own self-truth

There are, after all, priorities of killing rather than living.

I am taken to Churches and Cathedrals rich in history, reverence and bling. This, the land where two versions of the same orthodoxy compete for trade; patriarchs who speak one of two languages fire solemn soliloquies from the floor of these magnificent erections like PR men switch-selling brands.

Outside there are beggars; inside purple paint and glittering gold convincing the faithful – mainly women short skirted, see through bloused, shawled, singing and standing for hours – that they're in the right place. Or faith.

To more bars sharing the retro military theme; camo is the new black for street clothing. Where once true patriots of the underground hid, fought and lost their lives just seventy years ago citizens now concerned with the war in the East drink patriotic drinks and eat patriotic food to line the pockets of the patriotic entrepreneurs.

Do I seem cynical or dispirited? I am not.

This rich alluvial land has been lived on for forty four thousand years. This city I'm in has early medieval origins with beautiful buildings, cobbled streets, charming flag-stoned squares filled with smiling visitors. Yet earlier visitors brought swords and ponies, then horses and pikes and cannon and guns and tanks and aircraft. Ten times the uninvited arrived in the course of nine centuries.

Today, the phlegmatic population wants, like everyone else, food, shelter and procreation. They have fear, but it is just one more chapter in a thousand year story. It, too, will pass.

With my friends to their newer, larger and relocated motorcycle workshop; lights to be fixed and discussions on where to weld cradles to carry the petrol in cans for those countries with no roads or night-lit fuelling stations. Tall, strong, educated and eager to help, these men decide mutually to think about it further, to be fixed on my return in some weeks. I leave the cans, previously bungeed, a tent and sleeping and cooking gear which I will not need for some weeks, in a large cardboard box on the workshop floor.

We exchange stickers, manly hugs and heartfelt farewells when they escort as a convoy to the right road with no cobbles between. A final wave and I'm rolling north to some lakes on a road they do not recommend; but hey, I know it all.

The Rocky Horror Road

The experience of this un-recommended and lonely road of deep holes, ruts, mud, shale and sand was terrifying.

The motorcycle skipped, bucked, wove and fell continuously as if visited by the Four Horsemen simultaneously determined that they would hasten my end. After a while, on reaching a village, I stopped and started to shake from adrenalin overload. And smiled at fear defeated. It wasn't combat after all; and I chose to do this.

So I continued forward. Of course it got worse.

The road had taken a life of its own; between ten to twenty metres wide, top surface torn away by weather extremes, huge trucks and occasional cars cascading through transmission smothering puddles, lurching from the white painted trees that lined the road's perimeter to the opposite side to avoid the holes in the holes and collisions with each other. One hundred and fifty kilometres of unalloyed fear spread over five hours punctuated twice, to calm and fool the fools, with flat tarmac stretches of five kilometres apiece.

An undoubted and serious curdling of the brain took place, which, at one point, wanting to take a photograph, the internal chorus in my head said – take a picture of this rutted horror and the gods of the road will hurl you down to be trampled and crushed by a twenty tonne Kamaz truck.

I believed the voices; pictures not taken and life preserved.

To, after a tortuous road through a re-visioned and

impoverished ex-soviet city-paradise of crumbling apartments, fresh-wrecked roads and a bridge crossed twice, once by design and once in error, arrival was at a large and imposing faded grey and pink holiday hotel. Built for two hundred families; occupied now by three. And me.

The receptionist, a golden haired starlet beauty revealingly dressed, leaned forward in confidential closeness to reveal more, and said in sweetly accented tones of halting English 'Mmmm…Credit cards… Mmmm… nyet. Food mmmm breakfast and dinner. Coffee now?' It is not yet dinner and breakfast is tomorrow. 'Mmmm. The chef is not here tonight.'

From a lift that creaked with theatrical relish, to a door with a box attached and plenty of dents proving previous occupation and parties. Why, in a huge and empty hotel, was I marooned alone four storeys up? Perhaps the hordes were already in transit from somewhere else; rooms booked and ready to rock. If so, I saw them not.

A communal balcony off the beige painted corridor, wrapped in cream curtains of organza and/or recycled wedding dresses, led to smoking opportunities, or a suicide drop. Or perhaps both, the one death slower but dirtier than the other.

I sat and smoked, adrenalin and ears still ringing and thought, 'I'm OK, I'm alive'; it was worse than Mongolia but not quite as bad as Kazakhstan. Just.

Later exploring and finding a private dining room draped in gloom and dark green in which fellow guests were holding, apparently, a birthday party. Two uniformed waiters stood apart guarding a cake displayed on a large mahogany cabinet which was in fact, a recycled radiogram. A table set for four, goblets clean, shining and filled with dark red wine, plates of food appetisingly arrayed and only two people seated. I was invited to join. The woman, sixty in a land that aged people fast, and her thirty something male companion smiled and beckoned.

It felt and looked like a scene from a Dickens novel. Ms Faversham and a paid-for paramour. Hungry though I was, I smiled, nodded but decided not to tarry. Too often alcohol spoils promising relationships; the party for two was already pointing that way.

In search of food I left the hotel and found a small petrol station standing within the hotel grounds. Constructed from unpainted corrugated tin sheets it had long since ceased dispensing petrol but continued to earn a precarious living selling Snickers bars and Pepsi Cola. And sloping shelves covered with garish 'made in China' tourist tat; presumably the stock had been acquired from the gift shop, now closed, forlorn and empty, that stood in the hotel reception area.

No phone calls from the night manager to offer women seeking brief affairs in exchange for money; I slept soundly and repaired for breakfast – included in the £10 tariff – at the earliest oh eight hundred opening hour.

The dining room was closed. Instead, breakfast was on offer in what I took to be the staff canteen. Painted beige of course, ten metres square, tables spread with fading oil cloth covers, hard chairs and a grey looking soup for my delectation. Next to this, the inevitable cucumber and unsliced tomato, with optional ham. I find it extra-ordinary that in most of Eastern Europe you rarely see a pig in a field. Perhaps they're all still collectively farmed in Factory 27 and processed daily in their thousands.

In any case, the coffee smelt good, the black bread was fresh and outside later with a second cup, the sky was blue and the sun shone warmly.

Leaving the city I was lost only once, or maybe twice, but the compass heading was good and onward then through dark green forest, dappling of birch, golden wheat fields limited only by the far horizon on arrow straight firm surfaced roads. With a bend here and there for interest.

Coffee and a Bitch by the Lake

Lakeside resorts are very popular. Here are long sandy beaches, clean water and almost uniformly good weather. The resorts pepper the pine forests and surrounding villages contribute food, accommodation, inflatable beds, buckets, spades and karaoke bars. The people are young, old, fat, thin, suntanned, pink, shiny and sweating and mainly undressed. Just like an English seaside.

Hard liquor and beer is swilled, candy floss mountains devoured, the fragrance of which almost defeats the ever present smell of suntan oil.

In my reminiscing retro mood of the early sixties, this is Good Time! Rock 'n' Roll of questionable origin blares from every small shop and thirty five degrees of heat pooling the sweat in my leather jacket I tool the motorcycle slowly through the crowds looking for a room.

The more attractive establishments are full. Moreover they all have gravel entrances and parking so from fear of refusal and falling off I pass them up quite quickly. After a while a sun-beaten wooden sign nailed to a tree proclaims Otel rooms in a language I understand.

I turn into the road; dusty, then sand (O gods!) then gravel and ruts (O gods!) and finally a sign I think says reception. It is so, but first, for reasons of planning, a room full of washing machines has to be passed through. I think this is not, in local parlance anyway, unusual. Until later when I leave reception and realise I had entered through the laundry.

I showed no Western credit cards; merely shook money, mimed sleep and by making a soft susurrating sound indicated to staff and customers alike that I sought a small cottage on the beach in which to sleep.

There were smiles and some suppressed laughter. But those present had not seen me perform a full bacon and eggs for breakfast mime. Yet. It's been known to bring the house down.

Eventually a volunteer; young woman with standard issue blonde hair, suntanned everywhere, sporting a tie-down bra and shorts, offered to show me the accommodation. I followed her still wearing my hot and heavy Kevlar jeans, full EU and English health and safety approved and best brogue leather boots, in a cooler thirty four degrees to a gaily decorated hut on the beach. Seven pounds a night no breakfast to be included. With an offer of full board; three squares a day for an additional fiver. I took the hut and declined the food. I would find candyfloss sandwiches elsewhere.

Hard standing for the bike one hundred metres from the beach; no, I am not an adventure rider so I took out toiletries and change of clothes, dressed the bike in its best waterproof cover and walked back to the hut past the dance floor and café that was to be, later, my downfall.

Undressing and showering took a few moments and into beach attire. There are times, and increasingly so with age, that I wish full Edwardian coverall beachwear was still fashionable. This to disguise the gravitational display as my muscles atrophy and the skin slides south.

I see a woman floating at the shore, bikinied and full bodied in the water, reading from her mobile phone. I know that for many a mobile is like an umbilical cord to life; I am surprised at the disregard for danger.

Near her, two towels on which another woman sits. Surmising they are friends and starved as I am of conversation for several days I approach and say good afternoon and receive in return 'Hello, where are you from?'

A conversation starts, nationalities and locations identified, journeys compared; theirs from a university city some two hundred kilometres hence, mine seemingly from another planet. It is fun and gentle and they are leaving to go home that evening on the bus. We arrange to meet for a farewell coffee at the dance hall to which, in due course, I arrive. Clad now, of course, in brown leather jacket and aforesaid Kevlar and boots.

As seems customary these days, selfies were taken and a passing holidaymaker was suborned into snapping the obligatory full jump with all feet off the floor.

It was at this point my downfall occurred. The dance floor still empty and caught in the moment I rushed to the centre and, fully leathered and biker'd struck a John Travolta Saturday Night Fever pose.

Regrettably both of my companions were from the East of Europe and too young to have known, heard of or seen JT in Fever. Vaguely embarrassed smiles, hands extended and murmurs of buses to be found and travel to be undertaken and I was back unsurprisingly, alone on the beach on the veranda of my hut.

The beach was calm, empty and beautiful; sunset painted the water and as the moon rose the white sand gleamed softly. Offshore a couple paddled a canoe. I strolled to the water's edge and sitting on a beached boat in the shallows, watched them out of sight.

Back then to the café and the dance floor and a table of my own at which to eat and watch the assembly as they gyrate enthusiastically. A sort of strangulated twist with the occasional arm thrown and Fevered hand on hip stance. Enough came soon enough; the sounds of music quietening as I returned to the hut, lay down on the bed and drifted asleep listening to the waves of the lake.

In the bright sunshine of the early day I am back in the café and with confidence returning I look for last night's waitress to ask for black coffee with sugar. In this country, earlier and in another café, I learned that sugar was pronounced sakha.

Showing off to the waitress and trying to impress I asked for coffee but mispronounced *sakha* using instead the French *sucre*. The previously friendly waitress walked off in a huff. Not two weeks later, repeating the same mistake, I was told I had ordered – 'Coffee, bitch!'

The wonders of language once more displayed I went to the lakeside beach trying to change my skin colour from grey to gold in thirty minutes. It never works.

As I watched, several old women – the celebrated Babushkas – wearing headscarves and long skirts were pushing bicycles across the sand. Each one was laden with pastries or barbecued sweetcorn. I stepped up to buy, avoiding bitchiness by pointing and holding out money. The pastries were puffed and full of a minced meat and deliciously spiced. The corn, as always, just scrummy.

Although the bikes were heavily laden it was a remarkable change in delivery technology; just a couple of years ago similar women in the Black Sea resorts carried their wares in handmade wicker baskets returning to base for refills every ten minutes.

More now, and fresher. Capitalism works.

A word on my accommodation before I leave. For some time in England, Health and Safety and Building Regulations decreed that all new installations of electrical sockets must be at waist height. The builders of beach huts in this country are not going to be outdone. The sockets in mine are two metres high. I have to jump to plug anything in.

Two days' laziness comes to an end; panniers packed and fixed to the bike. Onward says the team in my head. And for once it's unanimous.

Keep Calm

I am in the capital city of the land with two languages at war with its neighbour. The sun shines, most people are happy; there is much road-kill so food presumably, is as plentiful as the lack of road skill.

On the way to the capital I was stopped to wait for a convoy. Huge military trucks, guns, rockets grinding along; it took an hour to pass. A definitive reminder that all was not well. Eight hundred kilometres east people are dying for one man's delusion of power. The nation is united in this war. And also because centrally produced hot water is not available for the duration; everyone is re-learning how to wash in a bagna.

I am told that a woman will marry you, no questions asked, if you have a boiler that works; or at least that can be fixed. Plumbers have preference over professors. Two wars ago it was nylon stockings, the last war Levi jeans, this war a boiler. Such is marital inflation.

Twenty four years ago I discovered the Net. Liked it, thought it had a future and searched worldwide for people with skill; I found the best in the world right here. As a consequence I set up and still own a couple of web and software development businesses here in the city.

All these years of commuting and I still cannot speak the language. In my defence, our contracts are in the west where English is the language of commerce. Our people are hired for technical and linguistic skill – so English is spoken most of the time. Although a most frequent visitor, I am rarely in country for more than seven days so have no time to learn, although I can almost order a salad in two languages. And, of course, I am English.

And I am thrice blessed because my business partner of eleven years speaks English fluently, is diligent and skilled and likes motorcycles too.

There is much in the city to excite. Medieval monasteries filled with mummified Saints, superb modern buildings juxtaposed with Tsarist palaces and crumbling Khrushchev apartments set in wooded oases. Gardens and borders are delineated with used car tyres and walls and fences all painted patriotic yellow and blue. There is no waste; recycling is paramount now.

But there is corruption still, on a huge scale.

Corruption in this country has caused two revolutions and a war. I have been present, in country to observe all of these events at first hand.

One Language as an Excuse for War

To the now, and coffee in a café on a broad boulevard edged by five-storey high grey stone and brick, built with the skill and sweat of prisoners of war. A story is told that the city was blown up and destroyed in World War II; it was blown up for certain but the question remains as to who actually blew it. The invaders from the west or the friends of the invaded from further east?

I don't know the answer to this question, but I do know this country's history since this café was raised from the ruins. The more so as I have been here, on and off, for the past two decades.

Stay with me now… Stay with me a while and I'll try to explain the deaths of thousands of innocent people, the movement of millions more and the rape of the country for billions and billions and billions of dollars.

Almost thirty years ago in 1985, Mr. Gorbachev, then President of the USSR, admitted that the economy was sliding downwards and living conditions had worsened; he was the first Soviet leader to have said it. He launched a new policy, appropriating the word Glasnost, meaning openness and transparency. Two years later the laws promoting Perestroika, meaning restructuring, were enacted. These laws were introduced to strengthen the socialist economy by moving the responsibility for production from Ministries to state enterprises. Ownership of the State enterprises was subsequently moved to and controlled by workers collectives. The change in law also permitted private ownership of businesses.

None of these changes helped the economy; in 1989 the USSR started to crumble from within. The Baltic countries, Poland, Ukraine and the nations of Central Asia slipped the yoke and became independent. By 1990 the Soviet economy was out of control; the Berlin wall fell and Germany was re-united.

Throughout Russia and Ukraine the workers now owned shares in their previously state owned enterprises. But with the opening of international trade, consumer products from the West became available and those of the Soviet enterprise were no longer wanted. The currency fell drastically; people lost a lifetime's savings; inflation bloomed.

Factories could not pay staff; they were given more shares in the company and product instead of money. The workers could not sell the product, they had no money. The factories gave away their land to the workers so they could grow food.

Most of the money in circulation was held or could be accessed by former members of the Communist Party and managers of State concerns. The workers, desperate for cash to live and having no clear understanding what to do with shares they'd been given, sold them for next to nothing. The era of the Oligarch had arrived.

In the West, Poland, the Baltics and Eastern Germany rebuilt and prospered on a democratic and capitalist basis by joining the European Union.

In Belarus, Central Asia, Russia and Ukraine, criminals and former members of the security services moved into the power vacuum; democracy was corrupted by the nascent oligarchs who bought votes and put their placemen into political power.

In Ukraine in 2004 the Presidential election had two main candidates – Viktor Yushchenko and Viktor Yanukovych. Yuschenko faced West, Yanukovich faced East. When Yanukovich was declared the winner Ukrainians revolted at what they saw as a rigged election.

I stood in Maidan, the largest square in Kiev, alongside the revolutionaries. I watched columns of young people dogtrotting through the streets with flares and banners. Across the nation millions of ordinary people, grandparents, parents, office and construction workers, students and teachers gathered for days and then weeks in protest.

Finally Ukraine's Supreme Court annulled the election; a revote was called for and Yuschenko won 52% to 44%. The Orange revolution came to an end with Yushchenko's inauguration in January 2005. Ukraine's economy picked up a little. The gangsters were subsumed into the official power structures and half of the oligarchs ruled the country through Yuschenko.

Corruption from the previous administration was exposed. A minister committed suicide twice. Journalists were murdered. But corruption remained rampant; from traffic police to civil servants and lowly paid judges, money bought favours.

Supermarkets and shopping malls were built and in the major cities people could buy western goods openly. But telecoms infrastructure, distribution, supermarkets, petrol stations were owned by the oligarchs. State companies were sold to political cronies; the oligarchs grew in wealth and power, competed solely amongst themselves and discouraged entrepreneurs and market competition.

The authorities in Belarus and Russia, whose elections were at best questionable, became extremely worried about a democratically elected Government on their doorstep. Especially as Ukraine's government and West-facing oligarchs were no longer in their direct control.

In 2010 Yanukovich, reportedly a convicted criminal, won the Presidential election. The leading opposition candidate, Yulia Tymoshenko was, and remained for some time, Prime Minister. She declared the vote was rigged; the Supreme Court agreed but she withdrew her objections (purportedly under pressure from exposure of alleged illegal and corrupt gas and oil negotiations with the Kremlin) and Yanukovich was inaugurated.

Yanukovich's government promptly arrested Tymoshenko who was subsequently convicted of embezzlement and abuse of power and fined $188 million.

With no opposition left to speak of, and his members of Parliament either cowed or corrupt, Yanukovich set about the systematic financial rape of the country. In two years he allegedly stole $32 billion whilst his son made the journey from being an unknown dentist to major banker in just one year. As the country's state revenue was $31 billion the enormity of his crimes became apparent.

His family and friends were installed in all the main positions of power. State security, police, army, Tax administration even the National bank. In Belarus and Russia, in the Central Asian countries, this was not particularly frowned upon. Their countries and governments are run the same way; personal enrichment at the expense of the people.

But note – Georgia was an exception. And in Georgia there was a war.

Meantime, for Yanukovich, greed began his downfall. He started to steal companies and cash from the gangsters and oligarchs. They became restive.

For the people there seemed little relief or way of change. There was no rule of law, bribery rife. Companies were raided by men in ski masks carrying Kalashnikovs. Computers removed, tax infractions discovered or created and the offer of jail or sale of the company for a pittance.

The previous President and Prime Minister had long sought membership of the EU. The people of Ukraine saw membership as an economic advantage, but more importantly the introduction of the rule of law and an end to corruption.

Yanukovich took the people down this path for a year; the EU was just around the corner. People stayed calm waiting for the Agreement to be signed. At the same time, with economy in dire straits, Ukraine needed massive loans to avoid a complete crash and EU was guaranteeing help if Ukraine would sign the Association Agreement. For Yanukovich personally the choice was the EU, or Russia with love.

A loan from the EU would start the path to membership and rule of law. One from Russia meant business as usual.

He chose Russia and signed a deal for five billion dollars. Students protested and were badly beaten by the police force. That was the final straw. The nation went back to the streets.

They massed once more in Maidan and all across the country. I stood with them, in temperatures of -32°C whilst they built a tent city manned by the same grandmothers, mothers and fathers, farmers from the countryside, industrial workers, IT experts, students.

It was called the revolution of Dignity. The people wanted an end to the corruption. They wanted a normal fear-free life. They wanted membership of the EU.

Under pressure from the man who feared revolution in his own country and had promised to lend him money, Yanukovich allegedly ordered the shooting of his own people as they protested peacefully in Maidan. It had been peaceful. I was there to see it.

The oligarchs and gangsters were not oblivious to the disturbance and saw their chance. They stopped supporting Yanukovich and let him run. He took his $32 billion and fled, not surprisingly to Russia where he lives still. Safe from the international arrest warrants subsequently issued.

And with his exit Mr Putin lost his hold on the country of Ukraine. He saw the EU step into the power vacuum, welcomed by the people. And along with the EU at his doorstep came the threat of NATO expansion.

Rule of law was not and is not welcome in Russia. The economy is pinned to gas and oil. Power is pinned to gas, oil and corruption. A state asset privatised by an oligarch or two, their lives and allegiance to their President.

You know already where this is going and the reason for the war.

Leaders of all countries need an enemy to blame. Mr Putin, threatened by real democracy, stripped of influence and control of 'his' buffer state needed an enemy to blame and an excuse to get started.

He found two.

He protested the ousting of Yanukovich and subsequent election of new President and Parliament as illegal.

And he said the new Ukrainian government had made Russian an illegal language. So he had to protect the Russian-speakers of Ukraine.

The men in unmarked green uniforms mobilised. First to Crimea and then to the industrial heart of Ukraine, Donbass, where strangely enough, Mr Yanukovich had his power base. And the killing and murder and mayhem began and continues.

I sit here now, thinking of greed, the men who authorise killings to protect themselves personally, not necessarily the good of the nation. I am thinking and writing in this café on Kreshatyk, the main thoroughfare in the city, just one hundred metres from Maidan where one hundred heroes died for the rule of law and democracy.

And how two languages, spoken by all, were given as the excuse for the ongoing death of thousands and the movement of millions.

I sit, remember and write. There are tears in my eyes.

Musical Entertainment

When I am here, in this city, I visit the opera regularly. I cannot understand the language in the street or those used in operas. But the singing and the orchestra is always first class, and most people still dress up. Last night a production of Madame Butterfly cheered me immensely. And the best seats in the house – circle, front – were all of eighteen euros.

I have dealt with corruption large and small, petty officials, business and political leaders. And watched the city, the Nation and the people change slowly but irrevocably for the better, for almost two decades.

Yet roads in the city are still and for the most part, famously awful. Driving skills are dire; and the rich especially, buy licenses without learning and pilot huge vehicles at speed wherever they want, with scant regard for law or people. The stories of pedestrians killed and court cases disappearing are legion. Money still buys judges and judgements at every level.

I've had to learn to love the roads as tests of skill and enjoyment, no longer shouting at drivers who may be carrying guns. In short, as the cliché has it, to live in the solution and not the problem.

My personal solution is to smile and shake hands; to be, as much as possible, a representative of England, of cricket and fair play and try to seek similarities of culture, not dwell on the supposed superiority of difference. Outdated? Old fashioned?

Perhaps. But I am happy in myself and with my behaviour and eschew the whining of expats.

Here in the now I've visited my office and worked with my team for several days. There was business to be done, decisions to be made but now I am released.

On this journey I have travelled as far to the east as time allows. I will return to England on a different route and ask my friends in the west who are storing my kit to send it, post haste, here.

The post does not haste sufficiently. The road beckons. The heading is southwest and the skies are still blue.

Time to leave.

A Policeman's Bravura Performance

Out of the city and the land is flat, wide and empty, from horizon to horizon. In the centre, a wide straight black road. These roads were built by an aggressive empire to move men and munitions directly. No time for curves or genteel views.

The national flag is a blue rectangle at the top, a yellow rectangle at the bottom representing the sky and the steppe of endless golden grass. It is still the same in the modern world.

The road drives the vista giving life to villages straddling motorways; cows, chickens and people crossing at will. One storey dwellings, painted blue and yellow and white, gold-topped churches, newly minted and shining in the sun. Petrol stations compete for attention every thirty minutes. Occasionally a larger town decorates the tarmac with a low rise strip of stores and cafés flashing neon next to mock medieval truck stops.

I am rescued halfway to the border by a knight who arrived on a Blackbird when I was lost in the deep south west. No GPS, petrol-soaked Google paper map long gone. Not only did he guide me for three hundred kilometres foiling traffic cops enroute, he stopped to help a biker who, having misread a bend, lay in the ditch in pain. First aid applied, ambulance summoned and met and we're up once more and running until the border divides our routes.

Helmet off I see he is strikingly handsome. Blonde, blue eyes and chiselled features. He'd make a good husband to some equally gorgeous woman. But that could mean he must stop riding his bike. So he won't be marrying soon, he says. With a handshake, manly hug and wave he leaves.

Ten minutes later, that's all it took, I am negotiating with a policeman about speed limits in the village and lack of insurance documents. The law is that I cannot be fined or arrested at the roadside. The policeman is to issue a Protocol – a document of the incident – and I am to appear in court and pay a fine. The policeman tells me the fine is two hundred euros. I know it is twenty.

I am tired, it is late and the light is going. One of my headlights is pointing two metres ahead at the ground and to the left, the other straight up at the sky. I do not want to ride in the dark.

I ask for the protocol.

He says there is a new law. I have to give him my licence, ride to the nearest town, pay the fine to a bank, direct to a Police account, get a receipt and on my return he will return my licence. I know this to be a lie.

I have two copies of my plastic licence, ordered in England for just this eventuality. I say, I will pay, give me the protocol.

He plays his trump. It is a bank holiday, the banks and offices are closed for two days. You cannot pay the protocol and cannot leave the country until it is paid.

Another lie, but a bravura performance. He probably has children waiting for supper.

I smile, ask him how much if I pay locally, to him. Fifty euros he says, twenty say I and we settle at twenty five. No he doesn't want hryvnia, hard currency only please. And a promise from me to buy insurance at the petrol station twenty kilometres hence. Because, he warns me, there are more policemen waiting, and less kind, or more expensive, than him.

So I do.

Onto the border city and a surprise in a commercial sense. There are handmaidens of joy in a layby. They look a little older than their sisters in the country to the west. Perhaps they have been transplanted and the journey tired them out.

Through the city, onto the border road. A newly built wood-crafted hotel beckons, bed and breakfast included for eighteen dollars the night. Exhausted, sleep comes quickly in the king size, king-sized bed.

Alphabet Soup

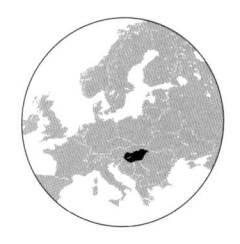

The morning to the border; low mountains, rain and mist. The road is mostly tolerable, the occasional ripped surface and repair aiding concentration.

I stop at a roadside café in the mountains. Good coffee served, a view of the town below and I watch a young couple, a boy and a girl in their twenties, hitchhiking east. They use the worldwide ploy. She in shorts showing a good leg, he in semi-hiding waiting for the stop. It works. In minutes a behemoth truck slows and stops in an extended hiss of air. She runs to the door, starts to climb in and then, with dislodgement and refusal impossible, waves for her man to join. The truck driver probably knew.

They leave, I leave. The sun has appeared and heats the road, steam rising in pockets. I'm rolling, the border appears on the down mountain side. Swift to exit, onward.

Now EU money sloshes everywhere. New, black and sporting six lanes, the road curves at a rush over bridges, through valleys, carved out hills. I am reminded in the first petrol station to purchase a ticket for this wild roller coaster ride. The car park is full of vehicles showing blue gold EU registration; it seems all twenty seven nations are represented, ready for the drive of their lives.

I have my entry ticket; we're off. No notice taken of speed limitation. At one hundred and sixty kilometres per hour I am assaulted from the rear by cars flashing lights… move over, move over, let me through. So I do.

At the side of the road is a green rag that has accompanied me for an hour. As I slow the rag refocuses into grass and trees and villages and I think, how stupid was that? Thrilling for certain, but this new country almost missed.

The green becomes golden and olive and I'm reminded of a room in my home. Where my grandson, the delight of my life, toddles the floor and climbs into my arms as we sit and I tell him stories. I am for a moment overcome with both joy and heart-stopping loneliness for my family, not seen for many weeks.

I approach a large city. The language here has Latin characters, with accents in profusion to confuse. An alphabet soup. Unlike the last which had backward Rs and snowflakes sprinkled about.

So I am still not sure of the name of this place. Buildings are large and range from cream to mainly light brown. They have an Empire stamp to them, and touch of the Hanseatic as I ride a huge bridge with flood water in a maelstrom below.

From memory (untrustworthy and dimming with age) I think my course is due south. It is after noon, the sun is overhead and a motorway appears to left of my shadow, ahead. South it is then, and three hundred kilometres more, then a border and bed.

Two petrol stops and I am at a border. This border does not have a name that I recognise. I ask a uniformed man. Ahhh, he says, that is this country's name as seen at the airport for the English. Here, and locally, we pronounce and spell it differently.

I am overwhelmed once more by the arrogance of my language. As a nation, in our past, we conquered countries and changed their names and spelling to suit our native tongue. And still assume that the natives we visit understand what we say. Fortunately, and due to better education and our American cousins flooding the world with a culture of sorts, they do.

I am on the right road, or at least the right country with the sun in my eyes at helmet level and an hour before dark with no lights. On a country road with glossy green hedges both sides I see large white rounded tents with pointy tops resembling, for me, alien spacecraft. I never did find out what they were and mention this only to say I was still wakeful when passing.

Now with Added Navigation

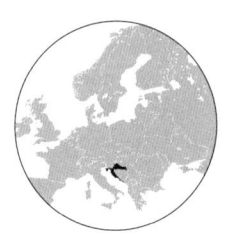

At the hour, as the sun goes down, I am in this country's second city at the house of my friend with coffee in hand as she cooks a welcome meal.

Not bad for a day's dead reckoning. Third country of the day, mountains surmounted and a customs man who readily forgave my English arrogance and lack of speech.

Once recovered a little we go, Tajana and I, to her mother whom I first met in Volume II. Tajana is a singer of jazz, with a deep, smoky, chocolatey and soulful voice, who makes a living as teacher of tots.

Her mother still retains the good looks of youth. We flirt outrageously and cry with laughter. She makes a suggestion, which I take up, to navigate onward with dice; it would be, she said, no harder than now. Hooray I cry, taking up the dice she's handing me. No longer washed out Google maps, or any maps or faulty GPS. The sun in the sky, a roll of the die; my life transformed again.

To protect Tajana's good reputation, when I am here in her home, she stays at her mother's and I sleep in her apartment alone. The motorcycle is garaged to deter thieves and plans made to visit nature, in abundance, at dawn.

Dawn, and I am still asleep.

At the door loud knocking, key turning and Tajana and Silvija – another long-missed friend, here to guide me past unexploded ordnance in minefields from the recent civil war, to lakes ignored, untouched for years and a tiny tourist village.

We've passed safely through the minefields with skull and crossbones warnings. People still die when walking in the forest; the ordnance still waiting to be cleared.

An old diesel powered paddle boat is tied up to small and rickety jetty at the water's edge. We board on the gangplank, the engine clatters to life and we set sail on the dark green lake of one of the largest areas of wetland in Europe.

Willows are half submerged, poplar, oak and elm in profusion dominate the higher ground. Storks and cormorants slide through the air. I am told a story that the cormorants are from China, centuries ago, and once used for fishing too. Now, when they colonise a tree it will die within seven years; the effluvia of cormorants too strong and intense for the tree to continue life.

We sail into deeper silence broken by the engine's alien clanking. The birds are not disturbed and continue to dive and fish. Carp, pike, catfish and perch. Occasionally a flash of silver as a bird's prey is tossed for better positioning and then swallowed whole.

We talked as we sailed as we had before, about civil and religious strife that tore the region apart just a few years back. It was like this, Tajana said and Silvija agreed: After the old dictator died, Statelets appeared along largely ethnic and linguistic lines. A power hungry politician stood up and said 'have you heard what they're calling us next door? It is an insult. Let's drive their people from our land and kill & maim them too'. Another politician, in the country next door then stood up; 'have you heard what they're calling us next door? Let's get rid of their ethnic types and kill and maim them all.'

And so it happened; people who had lived happily cheek by jowl for a century or more were driven off their land for religion, accent and anything else agreed upon at the time. When the madness was over thousands were tortured or dead. Distrust still loomed, gangsters and traffickers strong. NATO forces and EU money brought an acceptance of law, and peace has spread since then.

Strangely enough, two years earlier I heard the self-same tale in the self-same words from a Muslim in the country next door. Perhaps dictatorships holding ethnic groups together, are not then quite so bad; but when you look at the small man in the East it is hard to believe it so.

Trees overhung the still water, reflections like a mirror. Timeless. And after two hours, time to go.

A café on stilts over the water, Lavazza served and swallowed; so good a second cup is ordered all round and cherry pie an extra treat.

A visitor centre, small, brick-built and timbered in the style of centuries past, manages to sell Chinese tat though not to me, and then back to the car and onward on the road on top of the dyke.

The tiny village is accessed through a bar. Equally tiny shops, though reputed to be the size used in times gone past, are set up as butchers, bakers, candlestick makers; a school, smithy, stables, carpenters; all manner of things brought back to life and used, for the tourists, as they were two hundred years ago.

And I found it fascinating, absorbing and lots of fun. It was also of people empty, so everything was seen and touched and ooohed and aaahed with ease.

And on then to a deposed dictator's mansion in the forest. Dilapidated, virtually unknown, sad and somewhat small, for a man feared by millions. How soon reputations and expensive toys lose their glister. Hmmm. Motorcycles too.

Back to the city and I take my hosts to dinner in a café by the river; minimalist smart, the food good and the service unobtrusive. A simply beautiful, quiet day spent with good friends; but a thousand kilometres loomed. Goodnight and farewell said early, and so to bed.

Butterflies and Beautiful People

At oh eight hundred rolling. Lost by oh eight fifteen. The dice are deployed and by oh eight thirty the wheels are spinning past fields of gold on an empty motorway.

I can see, ahead and to my left, three witches' hats that morph into stand-alone mountains. It is the point in my journey where the confluence of roads, weather and speed has me biting my hand to roll off the throttle. In vain.

I'm sliding round sweepers at opposite lock then slowing for a diminutive shape, in the distance, walking the road. It is a man; beautiful of face, bearded, tanned from head to foot, loose limbed and walking with long comfortable strides. He is dressed in brown rags. He smiles at my passing and I am left wondering, as I accelerate away, if Jesus himself is alive and walking these roads.

Silver trees with sylvan leaves wave at my passing. The temperature has ticked up from fourteen to twenty-one. It is not yet ten o' clock.

I am not in Switzerland. I am in another new country; it is the country that Switzerland would like to be.

Snow covered mid-summer mountains. Wooden lodges and red-roofed white cottages dotted about. Deep valleys with turquoise rivers and lakes accessible from the road with ease and villages clean and polished and welcoming and serving coffee and cake, both delicious and cheap.

I know it's not Switzerland because of the price of coffee; an equally important clue is that serious circumflex accents shaped like butterflies now adorn the road signs.

Two years ago I stayed with a woman for a couple of days and nights in a small beautiful town sat on top of a gorge through which turquoise water flowed, smashing white on the rocks in its wake; the woman tended her garden by starlight while smoking a herb that made her smile. Most of the population seemingly smiled most of the time; who knows about the use of herbs?

Commerce had made itself felt, if not always in an endearing way.

At many petrol stations there seemed to be a tradition of cleaning motor car screens; and if you voluntarily paid, the rest of your vehicle too. The cleaning was done by beautiful girls in very short shorts; which though charming seemed somehow more demeaning than being washed by men with overalls on.

Mountains appeared on both sides of the road pulling me forward, new horizons appearing quickly. This journey this time was faster, limited now by need of the smooth tarmacadam that motorways provide.

Some uniformed men in a car park in the second country today told me a story about a vignette. We agreed it was both funny and sad that my understanding of the word vignette was different to theirs.

They had a smart van; computer, recorder, printer. Everything an agent of the State required. So, in appreciation of their story I gave them €150 and tarried no longer. Hey ho... soon to be in a country where I know what I'm being fined for.

A tunnel ahead, warm, dark; an umbilical cord to the next nation.

On emerging the sunshine is blinding, huge and snow-capped mountains surround and I'm into a road stop for food and a new and different vignette paid for in a different currency.

A car with Belgian plates has parked awkwardly behind me. This is not Belgium and the occupants dismounting are, after all, welcomed fellow travellers on the road. I see the size of man. Who is dwarfed moments later by a hippo masquerading as a woman with a headscarf and veil, blocking my exit and herself getting stuck between two cars. I think of Monty Python; residents of Belgium, La Grande Bouffe mobile and abroad and spread to more religions. I mount the curb and on the footpath, carefully leave them to wobble in my wake.

The grandeur of the mountains hold me in thrall, but in places, in passes with very tight turns, causes my stomach to seriously flip. Huge trucks crawl in convoy, impossible to overtake, mile upon mile of slow speed second gear grind.

Finally free, open roads and this country left, another under my spinning wheels. Small neat villages; red roofed. Larger towns with imposing medieval city walls, castles seen high surrounded by dark green pines.

I am eighty eight kilometres from tonight's destination. One thousand kilometres already done, dusted and folded neatly away.

So it rains.

Then pours and thunder roars and lightning flashes and I discover why flat rectangular plates are welded to posts every twenty metres at the side of the road. With a crash and blinding, a lightning flash grounds and strikes the plate to my right. A swell of energy hits me; the rain in torrents is boiling down the road and the bike is aquaplaning badly. Slowing, I find a petrol station, ease in under the canopy and pull up to the pump. Fill up the tank, pay and return to the bike, which repays me by refusing to start. Nothing. No hiccup, no lights.

Dead.

I am a small man. With petrol and panniers and tent and camping and luggage and compass sitting in the tank bag, the ensemble is almost too much to push to the side. It gets easier, once I have the found the neutral gear, but heavy just the same. A woman from the west and slightly north (by her hairstyle and demeanour and large Mercedes saloon) is shouting for me to move so that she can fill up and leave.

I struggle and sweat and pray and Justin (truly it is his name; the Travellers' adopted Saint), a fellow motorcyclist, arrives at my side to assist. Together we push, get clear of the pumps and together in English, though not his first language, compare notes on rain, breaking down, and impatient women. We drink coffee and smoke companionably before discussing the matter in hand. Bike, dead; complete and catastrophic electrical failure.

He turns the key. Lights, computer, ignition. Thank you God for all your Saints and this one more than most. He shakes my hand smiling, wishes me well, mounts a large BMW and is away in the lessening storm.

I mount up too, and at slower speeds to let water drain, I follow, but lose him ahead.

And lose myself in this city I aimed for. I have circled it three times without seeing the route I'm trying to remember. Rain still splashes down. It is dark. At the roadside sheltering under trees I decide to have a smoke for its calming influence. The lighter is soaked and won't work. My phone battery is at three percent and the charger is not working.

Dice are deployed in one last desperate attempt. Two kilometres with headlights failing I recognise my surroundings. In five more minutes I'm having coffee and pizza with the green eyed beauty with whom I stayed on the journey east.

We chat; of her former country to the east, green men and the subterfuge war. As an antidote I relate some of my journey. Smiling finally she goes to bed; I snuggle under blankets on the couch.

In the morning she has departed for work.

It's hard to get started. At seven a.m. I'm struggling to pull on still-soaking boots. Even the brogue bits looked forlorn. Thank goodness, say I, for waterproof socks. Just another thousand kilometres and this year's journey ends. Many wonderful hours with brilliant people, old friends revisited and a host of new ones made. Family await... especially my beloved and growing grandson.

Right then, stiffen the spine; onward, the next horizon.

Two hundred kilometres later in bright sunshine on well-surfaced roads, my body decides it needs to be fed.

Into another petrol station and as always, a small crowd gathered to look at the bike, ask questions and generally observe how long-distance bikers behave. I pulled on a jumper because although the sunshine was now bright and warm, at speed it starts to cool.

My preferred lunchtime diet, Snickers, sits open and waiting on my tankbag. Unfortunately the chocolate melts and slips down the tracks of the zip. The crowd is unimpressed and turns away as I lick my tank bag clean.

Some more mountains: below the tree line the forest turning gold; on the road I'm surrounded by travellers returning home at summer's end. For me six hundred and fifty uneventful kilometres to catch a ferry, over the sea and the final lap to home.

I knew I was a bit early in this, the third of today's country count.

For those that know it, it's the one where they don't even bother with words anymore. The roadside turns are shown as numbers. I can read numbers in Latin script. Neither Mongolian nor advanced Klingon is required. I've given up on dice, decide just to go with the flow – wherever the trucks head for, that's for me too.

It works. Another country, words return to signs and I know, more or less, where I am. And where I am, looking at my ticket, is one day earlier than I should be.

Journey's End

I'm sitting in the dark in a car park, smoking and casually cursing. I can curse profoundly in several languages, sometimes simultaneously, but as this was my own fault it was casual. Not even creative.

I'd done the self-same thing in Volume III. But that was a very long journey over several months where I first learned Mongolian and I could be forgiven for losing track of time.

I always buy a return ticket for the ferry back to England. It gives a time, a date, an ending.

My life is very flexible. I rarely have to be in a specific place at a specific time. I can operate my business from anywhere at any time. I like this and, apart from missing my family, it means I can usually go anywhere for as long as I like.

So. The ticket and the car park.

If I didn't buy a return ticket I could keep on going. And going. But I am not a rootless person. I don't have the psyche for endless travel. Even if there are years in between I like to have a beginning and an end.

I can only travel because I know there is love and a welcome waiting for me. It gives me fortitude when the bike is on the floor and I am struggling to pick it up. When I am cold and wet and exhausted and there seems to be no end in sight, I can gather the strength because I know I am loved.

And missed.

So the return was previously bought so I could get to journey's end and here I am, one day early for the ferry. At the control kiosk before customs I say to the young woman on duty 'I think I'm a little bit early' and smile what I thought to be a guileless smile. 'Norraproblem Sir' she responded '…normally. But you are a day, not simply an hour earlier, than you should be.'

'And I can't?' I asked, nodding towards the ferry preparing to leave, knowing the answer already and running out of words.

'No Sir. But you can buy a ticket for today from the counter if you like.' Said counter being a mile away. Off then, and round the corner, logging onto free wifi and buying a ticket online for the ship that sails in an hour. I had learned in Volume III that buying a ticket for the same day passage from the counter was four times the cost of buying the same online. I wrote down the ticketing code, returned to the kiosk, gave over the number and was told if I hurried I could catch the ferry about to depart.

Sea. And salt spray that extinguished the cigarette that I am only allowed to smoke in an open place. And remembering I had sworn to stop smoking before I set foot again on the green and pleasant land.

Too late. My foot is down.

Two petrol stops, the second at two, with a cup of proper English tea with milk, and I'm home at two thirty.

If the brass band had been there to welcome me they would have been too early too. I turned off the ignition, kicked down the stand and said thank you God sincerely and went upstairs to bed.

My wife woke up as I struggled in the dark and said, with love and a smile, 'Hello Darling, you're home a bit early. How nice.' And slid back into sleep.

Why I Travel by Motorcycle. Alone.

I think the desire to share experience and hope comes to us in later life. When you're young, you test your own limits. How far? How many? How fast?

I'm older now. It is people I travel to meet and share with.

I've been in combat; I have no desire to visit another country's combat zone to see if death is different. Equally I no longer have the physical strength to help shift a mountain of concrete caused by natural disaster. Hats off to those who do. I'd like to, but I know I'd be a hindrance more than help.

I do not seek off-road riding in dangerous environments. I am too old to bounce. Things crack or break. In any case, ride far enough and the off road comes to you.

Since my teens, I have travelled the world. The excitement of meeting new people and seeing new things is truly addictive. I learned, of course, that sailoring in the war machine restricts the type of people you'll meet. It's only sailors who believe that nice girls love a sailor. The nice girls' mums lock the nice girls up when the Fleet's in town.

You can fly to the sun with a group, but you'll mainly speak to each other. It's fun, but you'll generally come home none the wiser.

And whilst laying on a beach or throwing yourself off a mountain top is adventurous to some, it's not, for me at least, meeting and sharing cultural understanding.

But go by yourself, have the courage to put out your hand and say hello to a local and your world can turn in moment.

On a motorcycle you are vulnerable. It only has two wheels which can easily fall over. People know that. They'll be inquisitive and in your vulnerability they'll find you approachable. If you're in a group, even just two of you, you have a built-in support system. You'll probably manage without the local populace, you'll just skim the cultural surface.

And if you're dressed like Darth Vader on a bike designed for Judge Dredd, you'll probably learn very little indeed.

When I travel alone and something goes wrong, a mechanical fault, an accident, or just running out of petrol on a lonely road I have learned to welcome it. My experience is that I'm going to meet someone new who will help me, but more importantly give me a fresh perspective on their life and mine.

Travel, finding your own truth at first hand, is a very strong antidote to ignorance, prejudice and hatred. People everywhere want the same things: Food, a roof, peace and hope. Some, ambitious, want and achieve an extra room or car or home, but rarely at the direct expense of another human being.

A few people, with no compunction, want much more. They need people to bow. Or steal countries because they can. Wars start, millions die.

Then the people who start the wars die too. Achieving what exactly?

Wars cannot be fought without hatred. Hatred is learned. No-one is born with hatred in their heart. Hatred is taught and spread by people consumed with fear.

I travel, I see things unfold in front of me. I am a witness to that moment and understand that every story has two sides. My truth, and your truth, will be different from that of the media.

One mile at a time, we could do a lot to beat prejudice and hatred.

We live in a wonderful world, full of wonderful people. For all those people, who made my journey magical, including you, thank you.

Kit for the Journey

Much depends on where you're going and how you ride. I ride defensively no matter where I am. Outside of motorways, which are the safest roads in the world, I'm travelling slow enough to see what's around me and the next bend.

Which bike?
Who cares? If you can pick it up on your own it'll be ok. If you're going on a long journey get the cheapest and most reliable that you can. But don't expect a dealer network everywhere. DHL works. Losing or destroying £15,000 is a big hit. For £3,000 you won't worry so much.

Which tyres?
Depends on the bike but generally speaking dual sport are designed for 70% to 80% on tarmac and 20% off road. The best I've found so far are Conti TKC70. If you call head office in Germany they'll arrange for a set to be delivered to the nearest dealer at no extra cost. And, DHL works wherever you are.

You will probably have a puncture. Tiny pumps that work off your battery are good. Also, in the boondocks, it's hard to find a roadside tyre inflator.

Keep it simple, keep it small
Things that pack really small are usually better designed but

cost a bit more. The payback is less weight and more miles for your money.

It will rain

Pack wet weather gear. A Tucano Urbano two-piece suit can be rolled up and kept it your pocket. And now you have wet weather gear you don't need the Darth Vader suit. Make sure you have a spare pair of dry gloves.

It will get hot

I am not a health-and-safety kind of guy. When it gets hot I take clothes off. I wear bamboo flavoured T-shirts and underwear. They wick sweat, control temperature, wash and dry quickly and don't smell for a couple of days.

It will get cold

A mountaineering base layer is a must. An electric heated vest or jacket (and trousers too for me) will change your life on the road. The heated kit can be used as the insulation layer on or off the bike. Heated grips are a boon.

You'll probably fall off

I'm not health and safety, but neither am I stupid. From experience I know that Kevlar works. In jeans, in jackets. I wear a leather or a wax jacket; neither have armour. I've only lost skin when I haven't worn a jacket at all. I take two pairs of jeans. One to be worn, the other clean and waiting. The amount of Kevlar is dependent on the climate. I have broken my bones on the road. Armour wouldn't have saved my ribs or ankle.

You will run out of fuel

I carry a length of plastic tubing. It was my mother-in-law's catheter and I took it with me five years ago. It is a godsend;

almost any driver will give or sell you a litre of petrol.

You will be entertained

If you're on your own and not Darth Vader'd you will meet new people and you will be entertained. You don't always have to look like a saddle tramp, even if you are one. I was interviewed at length on TV in Russia. Magazines too. Pack a shirt to wear on these occasions. I rarely wear purpose-built motorcycle boots anymore since I discovered Sealskinz waterproof socks; these latter will keep you dry, but they take a while to dry out. Pack two pairs. If you're forced to go through rivers all boots will take in water. So I wear normal boots on and off the bike – just make sure there's some padding round the ankle. And have flip flops or boat shoes that pack tight.

You'll have to park your bike at night

In a city or camping in the boondocks you'll have to leave your bike at some time. Disc locks work and weigh less than chains. Use a bike cover and cover it. I have a cheap camo cover that hides the bike from prying eyes in almost all circumstances. And I can sleep under the cover if things are really tricky.

Camping

I use a one-man Lone Rider mini tent. It will fit inside a pannier. The mattress roll is from Alpkit and rolls up very small. Alpkit also sells high quality sleeping bags. Sleeping in cold weather is always worse than hot; invest in a good three or four season bag.

I have a very small multi-fuel stove. East of Germany it's hard to get gas containers and they will be a different fitting to anything you've bought in your home country; you have fuel in the petrol tank. A couple of aluminium pots is enough.

I used to take an Aeropress coffee maker and filters with me, but in Latvia, I was introduced to 'country coffee'. You just put the ground coffee into the cup, add sugar, pour on hot water and wait for gravity to sink the grounds. Yes of course I have ground coffee with me! Lavazzo is available almost anywhere. I have sugar because milk is not always available. Both are carried in resealable bags as they take up less room and are less prone to spillage.

I usually have a couple of packets of dried noodle meals and some packet soup for real emergencies. It's a good idea although I mainly eat in roadside cafés and petrol stations when I'm hustling along. Bread and soup are the mainstays and less likely to poison you.

You will get ill

I am not a doctor... always check for side effects! But the following work for me.

Most on road illness is of the stomach kind; bad food, bad water. Pack Immodium or similar for diarrhoea, a few sachets of Gaviscon gets rid of indigestion and heartburn (chewing gum and liquorice can help) quickly.

Antihistamine pills like Piriton are good for allergies and some strong painkillers are always handy.

First aid is a little different: at some point or other I've suffered from sunburn and heat burn, eye injuries, general cuts and abrasions and the occasional fracture. I take some antiseptic wipes, eye drops, Aloe Vera gel for burns, sunscreen, band aids, some crepe bandage and a couple of sterile gauze pads. Take large ones and cut them down if you need to. Safety pins and tweezers are useful.

I also pack, but thankfully have never had to use, adhesive closures for a large wound.

You might want to read up or practice some first aid. The Navy taught me; I still remember most of it.

Tools

Take any specialist tools needed for maintenance jobs; for example my Guzzi oil filter is a bit specialist and so is the tool to remove it. I take the oil wrench and a couple of filters. They're heavy, but it means I can do oil changes for at least 18,000 miles.

Along with oil I need to check the valve clearances every 6,000 miles. This I can do, so I take feeler gauges, a small spanner and small screwdriver too.

If you have a tool kit with the bike it will cover most small things but I also take a small selection of sockets with a driver, two or three spanners, an Allen key set, some Philips heads for the socket drive and a long screwdriver – this latter need in my case to adjust the front beam. And long-nose pliers, electrical tape and a handful of varied fuses.

Big tools, to remove wheels etc I leave at home. If it's that major I have a mobile phone or passing motorists.

Finally, don't forget the cable ties and duct tape… these will take care of a whole heap of bits that fall off.

Notes